Praise for
Do It Right the First Time...

"I love that so many brilliant experts came together to share their wisdom in *Do It Right the First Time*. The publishing industry can be overwhelming, but this book will help writers navigate the terrain and avoid many common mistakes. Bravo!"
—Stephanie Chandler, CEO, Nonfiction Authors Association

"*Do It Right the First Time: How to Write, Publish, and Market Your Bestseller* is a powerful anthology filled with tips, tricks, and techniques from industry experts who want only the best for your publishing experience."
—Jill Lublin, 4x best-selling author, international speaker, and master publicity strategist

"We started our author journey through self-publishing, a credible way to get your words into the world. With proper guidance, you can create a professional product that enhances your brand and delivers your message to the readers you serve. Valerie J. Lewis Coleman is a knowledgeable and skilled mentor who helps writers launch the best possible print and digital products. Many writers will benefit from the guidance she generously shares."
—Mindy Kiker and Jennifer Kochert, FlourishWriters co-founders

Other books in the Do It Right Series...

Write Your Bestseller

- Writing strategies from master storytellers
- How to transfer ideas from your head to paper
- Proven resources to accelerate your success

Publish and Market Your Bestseller

- Strategies to save thousands of dollars, hours of research, and tons of frustration
- Little-known secrets to get your books to readers
- Ways to generate multiple streams of income
- Proven resources to accelerate your success

Do It Right the First Time Workbook

With the volume of information shared in the three-book series, readers requested a workbook to capture aha moments, amazing discoveries, and action items. This spiral-bound book has questions, quotes, and quill space for you to move forward with your book projects. DoItTheFirstTime.com

For Kindle eBooks, visit https://amzn.to/3zeQ51j.

Do It Right the First Time: Conversations with Marketing Experts

Compiled by

Valerie J. Lewis Coleman

Published by
Pen of the Writer
PenOfTheWriter.com
Englewood, OH

Published by

Pen of the Writer
Englewood, OH
PenOfTheWriter.com

Library of Congress Control Number: 2022914262

ISBN-13: 979-8-9865108-2-8

Edited by Valerie J. Lewis Coleman of PenOfTheWriter.com and Sharahnne Gibbons of SomethingInComma.com

Printed in the United States of America

Table of Contents

Introduction

I am excited to serve you on your publishing journey with advice from over thirty experts. Combined, we have hundreds of years of industry experience to help you master self-publishing to make money. We want you to succeed.

For your convenience, this series is divided into the three major aspects of publishing: writing, publishing, and marketing. No matter where you are in the process, you will gain information, insight, and inspiration to accelerate your progress.

To further catapult your success, consolidate your notes, and capture your action items, the *Do It Right the First Time Workbook* complements the series with questions, quotes, and quilling space to capture the nuggets you plan to implement. Get your copy at <u>DoItTheFirstTime.com</u>.

May your fingers dance across the keyboard and your pen glide across the paper as the world makes room for your gift.

Valerie J. Lewis Coleman

Conversations with Marketing Experts

"Writing a book without promoting it is like
waving to someone in a dark room. You
know what you have done
but nobody else does."

— Madi Preda

Note: Content in the following interviews was
modified for readability.

Valerie J. Lewis Coleman

Intellectual Property for Authors: Entity Formation, Contracts, and Copyrights

Nakia Gray, Esq.

V: Joining me today is intellectual property attorney and business strategist, Nakia Gray. Nakia is responsible for helping entrepreneurs experience profit, protection, and peace of mind as they build the brand of their dreams. She owns and operates Gray Legal PC, an innovative law firm, uniquely designed for digital entrepreneurship.

You can find her as @nakiagrayesq on all social media platforms. The first lesson of this discussion is to make sure that your social media handles are the same. It's easier for you, show hosts, and readers.

Nakia, as an intellectual property attorney, you help entrepreneurs with entity formation, contracts, and copyrights. Regarding entity formation, what should authors know before they self-publish?

N: You almost always want to form a business entity. You want your business to be separate from you personally to protect you from liability. It also helps you appear more business-like and serious. If you're doing this as a business versus a hobby, the first thing is deciding what type of entity to choose. Am I going to be an LLC? Am I going to be a corporation or an S-Corp? There's no one size fits all; however, lots of people gravitate toward the LLC, which is fine for many published authors. For some, it may not be the best option. It depends on the type of business, and the anticipated revenue. Are you going to hire employees? Is this business a full-time gig providing your paycheck? And there's all types of tax considerations.

So, before you decide on the type of entity, talk to a lawyer and your financial advisor. All my clients will tell you that they've heard me say a million times, "I am not a tax professional." That is not my area of expertise, so you need to get advice from the right people. Sometimes the advice may conflict since I'm giving the legal perspective, and theirs is about taxes and money.

V: I filed an LLC for the purpose of keeping my business and personal assets separate, protect my company name under the state registration, and to be positioned as a business not just a hobby. You said something about revenue earning. Is there a cap on income earning with an LLC?

N: There's not an income cap. The biggest difference between an LLC and incorporating is that an LLC is what we call a disregarded entity. From the IRS perspective, it's no different than being an individual. For example, when you file your taxes, you use Schedule C to list your revenue and expenses. Because of that, you have to pay self-employment tax. When you work for an employer, you have a W2. They deduct FICA, social security, and other things on your behalf.

But when you are self-employed, you're not paying into FICA or social security. So, the IRS charges self-employment tax, which is captured on Schedule C and calculated based on your net profit.

How can you avoid that tax? If you are an S-Corp or corporation. The S part is an election. It's a piece of paper you file with the IRS that allows you to be taxed differently and not double taxed, which is what happens in a corporation. With the S election, you are permitted to take what is defined as a reasonable salary. As a W2 employee, you pay FICA and social security to get your taxes out of the way. Since my expertise is law, I encourage you to hire a tax person to run the numbers to determine which business entity is best for you. Where am I going to legally keep most of my money? When you are an LLC, you are not on salary. You take draws and you're taxed on that. Check with your tax professional, but when you get to an annual salary around $250,000, the best type of entity may shift.

Depending on your state, you may be able to apply the S election to your LLC. Check with your tax professional because there might be a way for you to stay an LLC, but get the benefits of an S-Corp.

V: That's good to know. It's important to know, too, that entity filing is based on your state's laws.

N: Both. Federal with the IRS and state. Some states don't have personal income tax.

V: Like Texas.

N: And Delaware.

V: We work hard for our money and want to keep as much of it—legally—as we can. I'm not trying to get in trouble with Uncle Sam, Aunt Sally, or any other government agency.

Many of my clients want to tell their life story to help others, whether molestation, domestic violence, or just how to live your best life. I am often asked, "Can I be sued for writing about real people?" Nakia, how can writers use real people in their writing without, let me repeat, without getting sued.

N: This is such a popular topic. Not a month goes by that someone doesn't ask me this. Let me start by saying the advice that I am giving is not necessarily going to prevent you from getting sued because anybody can sue anybody. Let's talk about the best way for you to be successful and overcome a lawsuit if one arises.

When it comes to telling your story, there is a balance with the First Amendment. I don't care if you went to law school, everybody knows—even my kids love to tell me— "I have a First Amendment right to say what I want to say."

Yes. You have a constitutional right to tell whatever you want. You have freedom of expression. You can say what you want to say. You can tell your story. However, people also have the right to privacy. You can tell your story, but you don't have to throw me in it and put out my business. I have the right to keep my stuff to myself. So, that's the balance the courts look at to determine how much of your First Amendment right to freedom of expression can be done without impeding on someone else's right to privacy. They also have the right to not be viewed in a false light.

Whenever people are trying to tell their stories and they have things they want to share, the number one thing is: *Is this info out there already?* If so, you're not outing the person. If we're talking about domestic violence or rape, was there a lawsuit? Were criminal charges filed? What do we know about criminal charges? They are public record. So, if people know that this person was accused of raping or physically assaulting you by Googling their name in the state's criminal records, then you didn't tell anything that wasn't already told.

The other option is asking permission and getting a release to tell your story. I have done that for clients. Sometimes, parents are okay with telling your story of childhood trauma as part of your healing process. The first, and best way, is to get permission and have them sign a release.

V: In writing.

N: In a contract.

V: With their signature.

N: With their signature. And it's clear in the contract, whether there is compensation.

V: Because you ended up on Oprah's couch or Tamron's chair, and now they want money.

N: Exactly. So, take those into consideration. I had a client recently who had been through a lot with her kids' fathers. She's trying to tell her story, name them, and drag them through the mud. She can do it. She has the right to tell her story, but the fathers have a right to not have their business in the streets. It's a weird, tricky situation, especially if the person has a business or professional reputation that could be damaged by her story. You better be ready for a lawsuit.

V: Like you said, that doesn't mean they're going to win. But your money, resources, and time are tied up into fighting this lawsuit.

N: Yes. And as a brand lawyer, I'm always thinking bigger picture and what it does to your brand. Do you want the hype and buzz for your book overshadowed by a lawsuit? How important is that to you? The energy that you put into fighting with someone could put a damper on things.

I said all that to say that it doesn't mean you can't tell your story. You can use fictitious names and non-identifying information to tell your story without naming and claiming someone else. If you can do that, and it doesn't take away from the message, I encourage you to do that.

V: And then the disclaimer that states names, characters, and places are fictitious. Two things you said triggered me. My first book, *Blended Families: An Anthology,* is about navigating life in stepfamilies. When I married my husband, he had three kids, I had two. Not the Brady Bunch. Twelve years into the marriage, I was ready to walk away. Instead of running—or going to jail—I compiled my first anthology. More than thirty writers shared their perspective on life in a stepfamily. I told my story as a stepmother without mentioning the names of my husband's ex-wife and children. As a result, thousands of families on six of seven continents have been helped.

I encourage clients to consider telling the story as creative nonfiction. Change the names and add a disclaimer in the front matter.

I am not an attorney I just play one on TV. However, I often get questioned about copyright and copyright infringement. Can you give us a definition of copyright and its benefits?

N: Copyright is one of my favorite topics because it is our ability to have exclusive control over things we create. I also do trademark law. People often confuse copyrights and trademarks. Copyright protects the creative content we create. Any and everything you create including your books, poems, blog articles, course content, audios, and videos. Everything you create that's in a tangible medium form is protected by copyright from the moment you create it. However, I strongly encourage you, especially when you are publishing, to take it a step further. File your work with the US Copyright Office to get a copyright registration for that work. That's your proof that you were the original author. You have exclusive rights. No one else has the right to republish or use your copyrighted work without your permission.

Copyright infringement comes into play probably more often in nonfiction than fiction. If you take from other people without their permission while writing educational pieces, it can be very dangerous. The law doesn't care about your intention. Ignorance is not a defense. Another misconception is people saying that they didn't make any money from it. It's not about that.

My favorite artist is Beyoncé. I want to share her with everybody. If I download her project and make CDs to sell or give away, my intent is good; however, I'm infringing on her copyright, and she is going to sue me. When creating, for everything that didn't originate from you, ask yourself: who created it, and do I have the permission to use it?

Some exceptions to the copyright laws are a gray area. For example, if you're giving a little snippet for the purpose of educating or delivering news, then you might fall under fair use. You cannot take a whole chapter from somebody's book and slap it in yours.

V: What about Clip Art? Just because you bought Microsoft Word doesn't mean you paid for the right to use Clip Art, right?

N: Right. Clip Art stock images, stock photos, images of people, any kind of image that you didn't create, cannot be used without permission. Lots of people are creating with Canva — a wonderful platform — however, read the fine print. You don't have a right to those images. Even on sites where people buy the images like BigStockPhoto.com or IStockPhoto.com. You still have to read the license agreement because some of the images are marked for personal use only. Without a commercial license, and commercial means you can use it for selling or associate it with your business, you have to be careful. Copyright infringement is a big deal.

V: You mentioned fair use and being able to use some portion where the area is gray. Say I take three bullet points from somebody's website and put it into a book. I cite the source, the website, and the day I accessed the content in a footnote or endnote. Is that acceptable?

N: It's better than nothing. I'm glad you asked that question. Often, people think if you give credit, then that cures it. Not true. That's better than not crediting, but the best thing to do is get a release. They may have terms of use on their site, and it says you cannot take anything from my site.

Some people have what we call a permissions policy, which may indicate that you can take anything from the website, as long as you give credit, and this is how it must be credited. If they have that on the site and you follow the requirements, you're good. But if they don't, then you should not take anything from their site.

You can summarize, paraphrase, and recreate findings in your own words, but you cannot take the exact content created by someone else. You see the difference?

V: Yes. Otherwise, it's plagiarism.

N: Exactly. Just because you credit doesn't mean you're permitted to use it. If you're going to take something from someone's site, it is best to explain that you're writing a book and want to feature a specific part of their work. If they're okay with it, send a release.

V: I have a friend who had a business website. She hired someone to create the website, unbeknownst to her the web designer pulled images from random websites, but she didn't buy them. As you know, images have embedded code. A year or so after her site was live, she got a letter from a company.

N: Demanding money.

V: Thousands of dollars. She called the web designer who said, "You paid me to make the website. You should have given me images." Um, you should have told her to give you images. You're the expert and she relied on your expertise to do it right the first time. She could have bought images for $12.

N: I'm so glad you brought this up. How could your friend have avoided that? For everybody you hire to create anything for you, there should be a contract. That contract should have a clause that says who is providing images. And the designer warrants that they have the right to use images and content.

Indemnification means somebody else will take the rap for issues. With an indemnification clause, your friend could have passed the liability to the web designer. Any time you will have editors, designers, or illustrators, you have to be careful. Even cover art and book design, you have to have a contract to protect yourself. Because if somebody was ripped off, they're not going after them, they're coming after you.

V: Scary. You spoke about brand. Let me tell you my brand story. As an adjunct professor at a local college, I was asked to speak at a women's conference on campus. The keynote speaker was an internationally known author who had movies based on her books. She didn't fulfill her obligations to the college and changed her flight to leave early. Awful.

I asked her to autograph the books I purchased and take a picture with me. Apparently, she was not feeling me or my request. Do you know that chick bopped me in the head like I needed a V8?

N: No way.

V: Let me tell you, it's a good thing I'm left-brain dominant. I went into critical-thinking mode. Let me rewind to see if that chick hit me. Then I went through a mental checklist. If I hit her back, Jesus will be disappointed. My pastor will be disappointed. She's about the age of my mother, so that's not good. It'd be like knocking out my mother. I might lose my job at the school. And then my brand as an author. All of those scenarios ran through my head in a few seconds. I apologized for inconveniencing her and left.

I mentioned it to an attorney friend. He said, "You should have knocked her out. We would have gotten paid for sure." Possibly, but I don't know if that money would have been substantial enough for me to feel okay with myself, my integrity, and my brand. I knocked her out and got paid, but her bazillion followers hate me.

N: Right.

V: You have to protect that brand. Other than Clip Art, what else cannot be copyrighted?

N: Clip Art can, just not by you. Copyright protects whoever created it. You can't copyright someone else's work. You can't copyright something that you create that includes someone else's work. In other words, anything that you didn't create completely by yourself cannot be copyrighted without a contract. The way that we do that is by having a license agreement, work-for-hire, or co-collaboration agreement.

I had two best friends who were not best friends with each other. They co-authored a book, but one person didn't view it as a coauthor. They did not define who was doing what and now they're in litigation. Whenever someone contributes to the work, it becomes a new work. The finished product is a compilation of multiple pieces of copyright. The illustrator had something to do with it, editors, and you may have more than one author. Making sure that you have permission to use each piece comes up often.

V: I often see song lyrics in my clients' manuscripts: the entire song, the reprise, or a verse. When I tell them that they cannot use it—

N: That's copyright infringement.

V: Right. They'll say that it fits so perfect there and someone on social media "verified" that they can use it.

All these "experts" on social media telling people that they can use two lines. No, you can't use two lines. From my understanding, you can use the name of the artist, the name of the song, the project that the song was on, and the year it released. Is that right, Nakia?

N: There you go. The two-line thing is not a hard-and-fast rule. It's what people think is enough to not get caught, but it depends on the two lines. When you look at copyright, look at the whole. If a song has 500 lines and you used two of them, you might be okay. But if the two lines that you chose are significant in terms of what that song is about and how it was identified, then you could be in trouble. Don't follow that two-line rule.

V: It's not worth it. Like I tell my clients, "You're a writer. Get creative. Rewrite those words in your voice."

N: Give your synopsis. Give your opinion on how you interpret it. "I listened to this song and here's what it meant to me." No one can stop you from doing that.

V: Here's how it made me feel.

N: Exactly.

V: I had a client hire me to get her children's book to be an Amazon Top 100 bestseller. I noticed her manuscript violated copyright laws by including song lyrics. I explained that I didn't want to blast her out to the world for her to get sued. Although the originator was deceased, his family is still alive. Copyright lasts fifty years?

N: Twenty plus. The same thing goes for trademarks. You cannot put other people's brands in your book. Coca Cola is a trademark, so you can't mention it in your book.

V: Really? I can't say, "I went to Panera Bread?"

N: It depends on what is said afterwards.

V: Why is it necessary to include disclaimers in fiction and nonfiction works?

N: Whenever you're worried about that false light or someone being identified, you want to make it clear with a disclaimer. When it comes to nonfiction, recall my disclaimer earlier. I'm not a tax professional and you said that you're not a lawyer, but you just play one on TV.

In nonfiction you want to make it clear. I am not this. I am not that. And if you are this or that…. I am a lawyer. Any time I produce anything, eBooks, courses, webinars, or whatever, I say, "I am giving general advice. I am not acting as your lawyer."

I don't know your specific situation, so I need a disclaimer. Even if you are an engineer, and you're writing a book on engineering, you don't know every situation or person who's going to read your book. Since there are exceptions to every rule, include your disclaimer. You need a disclaimer to say that you're giving what you're giving as general education and information. However, it is not tailored to any specific person. Things change. Laws even change books. My son is in high school. He's reading books that I read in school, but lots has changed.

You need disclaimers because you don't want someone to say that they relied on your advice, and now they owe the IRS $500,000!

V: In April, I did a Facebook Live because people were asking me tax questions. I prefaced it at the very beginning, and several times during, "I am not a tax expert. This information works for me. You need to consult with a tax professional who knows your specific needs and expectations to work with you."

I explained how I use Schedules C and SE from my perspective and reiterated several times to go consult a tax expert.

N: We live in a litigious society. People love to sue people. And more than suing, people love to cancel people and blast them on social media. So, when we talk about your brand, even if they don't sue you, they'll go on Facebook or Instagram, where they have hundreds of thousands of followers, and tell them that you're a scam artist.

The court of public opinion or the court of social media can destroy you. You have to be on your p's and q's to recognize that people are always looking for somebody to blame. Don't let that someone be you.

If you're writing fiction, then make it clear that these characters, places, and situations are fictitious. Even down to the city or corner bar. What happens when the bar owner says that people think the bar rape you mentioned happened in his venue and now business is down? That's why you want to have those disclaimers in fiction.

And I cannot stress it enough for nonfiction. Even if you're telling your story, are you giving business advice? It's impossible for me to give business advice and not say something about taxes, marketing, and other parts of the business. But I'm not an expert in those areas.

What works for this hairstylist may be a very different situation for a doctor in California. I don't have any control over who reads the book, so I need to have disclaimers there.

V: It's good to know these things, especially for aspiring authors. What are some basic contract terms that every writer should know?

N: Which contract are we talking about?

V: A contract with an editor.

N: Work-for-hire is a very important clause that every writer needs to know. Remember, with copyright, the creator owns the copyright. The way it gets from that creator to someone else is by a work made-for-hire agreement. So that means I pay you. I pay an editor to edit, but they are not getting any copyright ownership. But editing can turn into writing a whole chapter. With several added chapters, you're moving into ghostwriting. Without a work-for-hire clause, who owns those chapters? That is so important when you hire someone for editing, illustrations, images — any of those things.

This clause extends beyond your book to your website. Anytime anyone creates something for you, you need a work-for-hire clause in the service agreement or a separate contract.

V: What about a website like Fiverr with thousands of freelance service providers?

N: Great question. I want you to get very familiar with terms and conditions. Every website should have it, as it tells you how things work. Fiverr, Upwork, and all freelance websites, have terms and conditions for their services. They have embedded a work-for-hire clause, but my advice to my clients is not to rely on that.

Fiverr is here today. What happens in ten years when you're a bestseller or you're doing a second edition and Fiverr isn't around anymore? The person who did your cover says, "That's my work." Even with Fiverr's embedded clause, I have them sign an agreement. Don't let this scare you and make you think that you have to be on the lookout. Most people are on the up-and-up, they just want to get paid. They're not looking to keep up with you. However, you don't want to take the chance. You should have a standard work-for-hire template that you shoot over to the freelancer for signature before the project starts. They will sign it with no problem.

I work with clients who decide to option their

books for TV or film. The producer is not chancing the project by taking your word that you own it outright. No, no, no. They need to see that you own it. It's so much easier.

Maybe you're looking to get a traditional publishing deal. This happens often for self-published authors. Down the line, after years of hard work, a major publishing house is looking to add you to their roster. They want to see that you own the manuscript. You can show them your copyright registration. When they ask about the editors, you can show them the work-for-hire agreements. What about the designer? I hired John Doe from Fiverr.

Now you're scrambling to get all the pieces. You never know when your opportunity will come, so stay ready. The work-for-hire is the number one clause that you need to know and understand.

V: To help keep entrepreneurs out of the courtroom, you have customizable contracts, agreements, and policies that are instantly downloadable and tweakable. What offerings do you have that are specific for authors?

N: Work-for-hire agreement. Copyright-license agreement, which comes up when someone wants to use some of your work. You want to be able to fire off that licensing agreement right away. It works both ways. You may want to license someone else's work.

Releases, especially when you're telling your life

story. I recently had a client creating a devotional, very wonderful, successful book. She told me that before the Scripture in each chapter, she told a short story that included people in her life. Wait a minute. Did you get permission? She hadn't so she purchased a book release agreement. After she got written permission, she said that it was the best money she could have spent.

I know many authors who think small. This book is their passion, ministry, or something God placed on their hearts to do. Most times, they're not thinking about the business aspect or how big it can get, and it can get big. And when it gets big, people see dollar signs. People don't want to feel that you're capitalizing or winning off of them. It's so much harder to go back to get permission. I had to double back to get releases for a client because she had a publishing deal on the table. I had a client who lost a deal because she didn't have releases.

Having releases is great if you're doing podcasts, too. The great thing about content that you create is that it can be repurposed into something else.

I have a client who had a very successful podcast she started with a friend. We need to do a whole other book on friendships in business. They did very well until it ran its course. The season was done. One of the hosts wanted to convert the episodes into a book. She thought that she would just run and do it. And I said, "No, no, no." I wrote a contract to get her former partner's permission, and then we had to get releases from all of those guests. They signed up to be on the podcast, they didn't sign up to be in a book. The release template I sell deals with that. It states everything in the future, so you don't have to double back.

V: Do it right the first time. So that's in your *Before You Self-Publish: A Legal Crash Course for Writers and Authors* (Bit.ly/LegalPOWER). Do they have access to you and videos? Can they download documents or are you teaching through this process?

N: Both. It's a recorded mini course with step-by-step guidance to choosing an entity, and everything discussed today. They have access to downloadable worksheets, checklists, and resources that help you figure out which business entity you want. I address terms, privacy policies, and things you need if you're operating a website. Templates, contracts, license agreements, releases, and work-for-hire are available.

V: All to help writers and authors do it right the first time instead of having to backtrack and hope people agree to the terms.

N: Right. And when that opportunity comes from a traditional publisher or movie producer, you can confidently say that you have everything you need to close the deal.

V: Before the interview you mentioned that you work with authors to turn books into screenplays and films. You mentioned Tressa Smallwood. She spoke at my publishing conference in 2007. I met her in 2005 at the American Library Association's annual expo. She's doing big things. I recently saw one of her movies on TV. Her name was in the opening and closing credits as producer. That's powerful. I'm sure this process is very complicated with all the legalities and moving pieces. Can you give a brief summary of what it takes to go from book to screenplay?

N: It's not that complicated, actually. In the case of one of Tressa's movies, my client rewrote or adapted her book based on a contract with the producer.

Sometimes a producer may acquire the rights to something, and then contract with a writer — who may not be the author of the book — to create it from scratch. Some producers have no desire to write screenplays, so they hire a writer. We're going to see more independent film producers getting out content like self-published authors have been doing over the last fifteen years or so. We're seeing independent films on Hulu and Netflix. Some people just air on YouTube. The key is the content, contracts, and of course, copyright. Tressa is a little different because she's a unicorn as a writer and producer.

Making sure you have the copyright registered is critical. Every author, every writer, can monetize their gift.

I had a client who wrote and did a stage play. She had an agreement with a producer to adapt that stage play into film. I drafted the contract.

V: I hired a professional actor to produce my audiobook. We had a contract in place. He converted my bestselling novel, *The Forbidden Secrets of the Goody Box* (<u>TheGoodyBoxBook.com</u>), into script form for the audiobook. I ended up narrating a main character and several minors.

N: That's good. We didn't touch on audiobooks, but that's another form of copyright.

V: I need to file the audiobook with the copyright office at <u>Copyright.gov</u>?

N: Yes. The MP4 or audio files.

V: Per <u>ACX.com</u>'s requirements, each chapter is a different track. I have about thirty tracks.

N: Copyrighting an audiobook is the same way someone would do a music CD. And here's why. What happens if somebody downloads it and puts it on a website?

V: I don't want any of that. Someone unlawfully making money off of my work. I invested money into production, actors, and travel.

I am a creator and I feel some kind of way about bootleggers pirating somebody else's hard-earned time, energy, effort, and money.

In your experience, what is the biggest legal challenge for authors and how do you serve them to overcome it?

N: Fully understanding copyright. It's a word people kind of know, but they don't really understand. Like we just discussed how every new piece is a new form of copyright. When you first write your manuscript, you should copyright it by itself is one.

When you add the cover, images, illustrations, and other things, it's a new piece of work and another form of copyright. The audio version is another copyright. When you turn it into a movie, that's another one. Fully understanding all the players and the permissions that are required for the copyright is the biggest piece. The collaboration agreement sets forth how all the pieces play together. The agreement indicates you're doing this part, I'm doing this part, but I own it. Or the agreement may state that we're going to file a copyright registration that says you own 30% and I own 70%.

V: It's important to note that when you file a copyright, go to Copyright.gov. As of this printing, it's $65 to file. I have heard people say that they didn't want to spend money to copyright. Instead, they mailed the manuscript to themselves as proof of originality. First of all, if you can't afford $65, this is not the business for you.

N: Say that.

V: Secondly, mailing it to yourself has no validity. It's not going to stand up in court compared to someone who has a certificate from —

N: The Library of Congress. The reason why we register is for proof that you created it. When you mail it to yourself, that doesn't mean that you created it. You could have stolen it from somebody and then mailed it to yourself. They used to call that the poor man's copyright. We don't do that. We don't want to associate with anything called "poor man." So, file your copyright registration the right way.

V: Absolutely. Great advice. What is your favorite business resource applicable to authors and why?

N: I am in the nonfiction space a bit more than fiction. The Nonfiction Authors Association puts on an amazing conference every year virtually now, of course, and they have tons of great resources.

V: I spoke for them a couple years ago on self-publishing.

Nakia, I so appreciate your insight. The wealth of information you shared will help writers and authors avoid some legal issues. I learned so much. I have work to do. Jesus.

N: This was great.

Nakia Gray is an intellectual property attorney and business strategist who helps entrepreneurs experience profit, protection, and peace of mind as they build the brand of their dreams. She owns and operates Gray Legal, P.C., an innovative law firm uniquely designed for digital entrepreneurship. She was featured in the article *Lawyers Reinvent Themselves with Virtual Law Firms* by *The Daily Record Newspaper*. As the digital landscape evolves into an expansive marketplace, Nakia thrives on knowing that everything she does will help an entrepreneur write their own rules in business and life.

Connect with Nakia
NakiaGray.com
Facebook.com/NakiaGrayEsq
Linkedin.com/in/NakiaGrayEsq
InstaGram.com/NakiaGrayEsq
Twitter.com/NakiaGrayEsq

Nakia's Favorite Resource
NonfictionAuthorsAssociation.com puts on an amazing annual conference with tons of great resources.

Designing Your Bionic Bio

Tenita C. Johnson

V: Joining me today is best-selling author, playwright, and publisher, Tenita C. Johnson. Authors write better, thanks to this editorial guru and entrepreneur. As the founder and CEO of So It Is Written, Tenita collaborates with industry professionals to take manuscripts to the marketplace, positioning them for literary success. I met Tenita on Chocolate Pages Network, a social media platform for Black authors. We met in person when I presented at the Anointed Pen Conference, and we've been connected ever since. I speak at her events; she speaks at mine. We share business strategies and ideas. I am THE only person to present at all of her Red Ink Conferences, which she hosted in several major cities for six years.

Tenita, one of the most challenging aspects of publishing books for my clients is creating a bio that speaks to their brand, business, and book. It can be difficult to brag on yourself in such a way that you connect with your intended audience without sounding conceited, cocky, or corny. Why do you think people write bios that read like obituaries?

T: People are following the trend. They're looking at somebody else's bio and using it as a template. I tell people, "Don't start with 'born and raised', where you grew up, or 'accepted Christ at an early age'. No one cares and what does 'early age' mean? Is it eight or eighteen?" Your bio should not read like we're putting you in the ground.

When writing an obituary, the funeral home gives you a list of questions. Where was the deceased born? Who were their siblings, parents, spouse, children? Where did they work? Where did they go to school? Those things don't usually go in a professional bio.

V: Agreed. No one cares that you are the tenth of twenty-nine children. Or that you walked to school backwards in the snowstorm, uphill, both ways, unless it is relevant to the book. How important is a well-written bio for an author?

T: You have to think beyond the book. You're going to use the bio for the back matter and back cover. People are going to ask for that bio when you speak. That bio goes on your website, Amazon, and Facebook. You're going to use it everywhere, so it can't be boring. People should read your bio and want to book you to speak without personally knowing you.

V: I ask my clients, "How do you want to be introduced on the big stage? Who is the most important person you want to introduce you and what do you want them to say about you? Is the first thing you want them to say, 'Jane/John Doe was born in the back woods of Mississippi?'"

T: Think of it as being introduced at an award ceremony. You won an Oscar, Emmy, or literary award. How do you want the host to introduce you? Nobody cares where you were born. We need to know your accomplishments and the problems you solve with your book.

V: We have all experienced being born. You're not giving us anything of substance. The most important aspect of a bio is identifying what qualifies you to write this book. Is it life experience? Did you get a degree specific to the subject? Are you professionally trained or certified in this area? For many of my clients, it's life experience. If you're writing about bullying, then state that you were bullied at home, school, and the workplace. Maybe you contemplated and attempted suicide. That makes sense in a bio and adds value to your message.

T: Right. Many people want to write about overcoming depression, abuse, or molestation, but they don't want to mention it in their bio. Even though the bio is part of the book, you have to look at it as a separate living, breathing document. As you acquire awards, speaking engagements, books, and accolades, your bio will change.

V: I'm mentoring a lady who wants to republish her novel about mental health. She gave me her original bio. Because it needed to be developed, I sent her a questionnaire with poignant, thought-provoking questions. She did a good job answering the questions and I was able to compile an amazing bio. One of the best bios I have ever written.

She had experience from both sides of mental health: as a workplace professional and a consumer of services, but didn't want to include that in her bio. I explained that since her book is about mental health—a hot topic—it's better to be transparent and vulnerable. Readers will better connect with your message when they understand that you're writing what you know as opposed to chasing the next hot topic.

T: Right. People don't realize the doors that can open from somebody reading your bio. One of my clients grew up with a mother who was schizophrenic. He talked about the things that he endured. When he released his book, doors opened for him to speak at universities and shelters. Before he released the book, he didn't have those opportunities. But as a published author and someone who experienced mental illness, you become an expert.

V: That makes all the difference. Since hers is a novel, she has to be even more diligent to hone in on her personal experience. She preferred her original bio that stated I'm a writer. I love to write. I was born to write. Everything I write is spiritual.

T: Nooooooo!

V: That's a waste of back cover prime real estate.

T: It is.

V: When we started the process of republishing her second novel, she said that she wasn't making any sales. After the bio snafu, I asked if she wanted to know why. I explained that she was not connecting with her readers. They don't see her as a "touchable" person who's experienced what she's writing. Readers cannot connect with your message, until they connect with you. And if they don't connect with you, they're not going to buy your book.

If she had hired me to publish this novel as a QueenVPublishing.com title, further discussion would have been necessary. I gave her my recommendations, but implementation is at her discretion.

T: People think that they're just writing a book. No, you're building a brand. That bio, professional headshots, everything that complements the book, goes with your brand. They speak to how well or not-so-well your brand is put together. I can always identify an amateur author simply by reading the bio.

V: Your bio helps your posturing and how people perceive and receive you. How do you want to be remembered? You have to set the tone for your business and how you want people to think about you, your brand.

Your bio is a major marketing tool. I have several bios. I have one about romantic relationships based on *The Goody Box Book*. One about the book business, and I one for my children's books. If I'm speaking to a group of aspiring fiction authors, they may not care about the children's books. I have to be strategic. You have multiple bios, too. The one you have for editing…

T: [Laughing]

V: You know what I'm about to say. When you wrote your second book, *When the Smoke Clears*, you tried to use the editing bio for that book. When you sent it to me, you included an emoji and a comment about being fearful to hit send.

T: I knew you were going to tear it apart.

V: I said, "She knows this bio is not acceptable." I replied to the email with "Boooooooooo!"

T: That's a good point. Submit your bio to five to seven colleagues requesting their opinion.

V: Make sure those colleagues have great bios. Because sending it to people with obituaries as bios…

T: They won't care.

V: I struggle to write my own bios. I talked with an informal mentor, Mo Stegall. He said, "Coleman, your bio is a mess."

I thought it was pretty good, but it was too long. If an event host read it to the group, it would take three or four minutes. I didn't know how to condense my accomplishments, experience, and results. He took it, refined it, and laid it out. I loved what he did, so I rinsed and repeated his formula for my *The Forbidden Secrets of the Goody Box* bio.

The bios identify who I am, the problems I solve for my intended audience, and how I solve them. Transparency and vulnerability are essential to a powerful bio.

Why do you think authors hold back when it comes to sharing their journey?

T: Fear of judgment. I challenge my clients to do the opposite. Whatever you are scared of people picking apart or challenging you on—mental illness, molestation, rape, depression—put it up front. The attention span of people is that of a social media post. Someone reading your full bio may tune out after the first two or three sentences. But if you have something in common, they're more apt to buy your book or talk to you at the table. Because you're not just writing about it, but you've been through it.

V: That's a big difference. Some people teach how to write a book in forty-eight hours. From what I understand, the training is about Googling topics, determining what's hot, finding articles, rewording, and then bam! Publish a book. There's no integrity in only rephrasing other people's work and not adding original content.

They may be making a bunch of money off the strategy, but I don't work that way. My clients and I write about what we know and experienced to help others make better decisions and get results like we did.

T: Right. Even if you don't say it in your bio, it's assumed that since you wrote a book about a topic you experienced it on some level. Otherwise, how can you write about it candidly or vividly? It's inauthentic to write a book about depression if you've never been depressed or you don't know anybody who's depressed. Writing about it from a clinical standpoint is not good enough.

V: I agree. Regurgitated praise is not a good way to position yourself. We talked earlier about our friend, Chanelle Wilson (VisitBetterDaysCenter.com), who has changed our lives with her powerful emotional polarity technique (EPT). She is great at what she does. Guiding you to address issues with her mantra: find it, fix it, and forgive it. She helps me get results, so I refer people to her. If I purchased a book and discovered that the author had no experience in the subject, I wouldn't tell anybody else to buy the book. Authorship has an inferred transference of credibility as a celebrity and expert. What happens if a media person assumes you're a subject matter expert since you authored the book? They bring you on their radio or TV show. You can't answer the first question because you can't remember what you copied from somebody's website. Not to mention copyright infringement. Whatever you write, write from your heart.

T: It should be authentic. I write creative professional bios that differ from bios for CEOs of Fortune 500 companies. In corporate bios, you want to talk about where you've worked, your degrees, and results.

V: Like a resume.

T: Right. In paragraph form. In a more creative way, you have to think about how your story affects readers. They need to know that you are who you say you are 100% of the time.

V: The bio is such a valuable marketing tool. You can land media attention, paid speaking engagements, and sell more books because of it.

T: One of the number one mistakes—I have five number one mistakes—clients come to me after their book is published needing a bio and headshot ASAP.

V: They didn't have a bio on or in their book?

T: Neither. Some people publish with the back cover blank.

V: That is such a waste of money.

T: Fill the space.

V: If you do it right, when you're not there to sell your book, it will sell itself. I spend more time developing clients' title, subtitle, and back cover marketing copy, which includes the bio, synopsis, endorsements, and more. They often say, "I had no idea it takes this much work to publish a book." When they implement the strategies, they kill the game. One of my clients sold almost half of his inventory before he received his books.

In all my years of publishing clients through Queen V Publishing, Necci Headen Cooper outsold everybody on Amazon in two months. I said, "What are you doing to sell so many books?" She said, "I'm doing what you said to do." Keep doing it!

My focus is getting readers to buy directly from authors to generate more revenue, recoup expenses faster, and build your email list. Despite directing them to her website, some readers purchased from Amazon. She has five-star verified reviews for *My Prayer Is: Whispers and Wisdoms for the Heart.*

T: That's good.

V: Teachable! I love it. We mentioned a couple of things that should not be in the bio. What else should not be in a bio?

T: Your kids, pets, and spouse should not be mentioned. People fight me on this because family is important. But it's not a family bio. I don't get your husband and kids when you speak at my event. I get that they want to give honor.

V: Put it on the acknowledgement page.

T: Right. I've had people include their favorite pastime, favorite color, where they like to shop...

V: Where they like to shop? Girl, bye.

T: Hobbies. He loves fishing and he loves to golf in his spare time has nothing to do with the book.

V: I ask those questions in my questionnaire. Not so much for inclusion in the bio, but for me to get a better understanding of the person. A mentoring client, Tyrone Givens, hired me to help build his virtual brand. He had a great book, but he wasn't selling as many copies as he hoped. I gave him editorial suggestions and helped him reduce his retail price. His print costs were way too high, so his retail price was inflated. I showed him how to cut his print costs by $4 per book. I had strategies to reduce it another $3 per book, but he didn't want to make any further changes. I rewrote the synopsis and his bio and made suggestions on the cover image, elements, and formatting. The book, *The Bennu Project,* is about a post-apocalyptic, African heroine. It has sci-fi elements and African history that he researched. He even learned several African languages to further enforce his message. He created the book because he couldn't find anything in African or African American history that was relevant and interesting for his homeschooled sons to read.

In the questionnaire, he indicated that he liked video games and flying. He wrote this book based on his passions. It made sense to mention that he was a federally-licensed pilot since his book had high-tech space crafts in it. He said, "That's not a big deal. It only took x hours of training and flight time." I said, "Sir, you are the only chocolate federally-licensed private airplane pilot I know. Do you know of any others?" When you do things well, you don't always consider them a big deal.

When he crafted these fictitious flying machines, he used his knowledge and experience to create them. He implemented my changes, and I distributed a media release. I got more responses from reporters than I had ever received. "I have to have him on my show. When is he available?" The bio, synopsis, and media release spoke to his credentials, qualifications, and reasons he wrote the book. He got nervous about the in-studio interviews, so I trained him.

T: People are taught not to brag on themselves, but to let others speak well of us. I tell my clients to write answers to common interview questions. Ask your social-media tribe, what one word comes to mind when you think about me or in what subject do you consider me to be an expert? If you don't consider yourself an expert, somebody sees you as one. You are probably undercharging for your expertise, if you're charging at all.

V: In my experience with Christianity and African American women, we're taught to be humble, submissive. You don't brag on yourself. That's not Christlike. That's not godly. That's not ladylike. I can brag on my sons all day. I can brag on Tenita. I can brag on my clients, but for me to write a brag sheet about myself, it's hard to capture my accomplishments into succinct, powerful words.

T: Very hard.

V: Hire someone who writes great bios, not obituaries, bios. Don't think about going to the casket think about going to the big stage. It makes all the difference in the world. What else should not be in the bio?

T: Most readers don't care that you graduated from high school.

V: Or with a GED.

T: Right. It's not a great life accomplishment. The average American has graduated from high school.

V: The below average person has graduated.

T: Right. I tell people not to include it in the bio if it's not relevant to the book. We can add it at the very end if you insist. I have a bachelor's, I have a master's, but if it's not relevant to the book, we can omit it.

V: Absolutely. I have an undergraduate degree in engineering, a master's degree in business administration, and I'm working on a doctorate degree in divinity. I don't put any of that on my book because it is not relevant to the message. You have a small amount of space to compel someone to know, like, and trust you enough to invest in your book. Don't waste space with unimportant information.

I had a client who wanted to list four or five sermon titles in the back cover bio. I asked if he received national recognition or spoke on the stage with a mega-church pastor. Nope. They were his favorite Sunday-morning messages. What makes you feel warm and fuzzy, doesn't always sell books. I explained that sermon titles do not belong on the back cover. If space permits, I may add them to the interior bio. He was a traveling pastor who didn't have a physical location. A pastor without a flock. Isn't that an evangelist, apostle, or teacher?

T: Right. Don't put the places you've worked, unless it's relative to the book. Your bio is not a resume.

V: So, not when/where you were born, not your birth order, not your parents, spouse, kids, or pets. Not your hobbies or degrees, unless they are relevant to what you're writing. If you have an earned doctorate degree, your bio needs to indicate that. A level of credibility is attached to earning an advanced degree. So, if you have a MD, PhD, EdD, DDiv include it.

T: Some people with honorary doctorates want to put it in bio.

V: If it's noted as honorary; otherwise, it's deceiving. Several of my clients have doctorate degrees and I incorporate that into the bio. We talked about what should not be in a bio. What things must be in every bio?

T: Write it in third person, not first. For example, "Valerie J. Lewis Coleman is a state-of-the-art publishing professional" versus "I am a state-of-the-art publishing professional." The former is third person; the latter is first. Think about your bio from the perspective of someone reading it to introduce you. You sent it to them with pronouns I, me, and my. They're standing before a live audience trying to convert it to she, her, and Valerie.

Next, capture who you are and your passion as it relates to the book. If your passion is transforming lives by helping people overcome depression, molestation, or whatever, your passion needs to be upfront. People need to know that the message of this book is pivotal and important to you.

V: That's how you help people transform their lives because you experienced transformation first. I was there; I went through this. Now I'm here and

I'm helping people experience the breakthrough, the transformation, the shift that I experienced.

T: Yes. It's the difference between transactional, "I'm selling a book" and transforming lives. What you write should be life changing. Don't write books just to write books.

V: Even novels.

T: Yes. Novels have an underlying theme or takeaway for readers. What makes you stand out as it relates to your subject matter? What qualifies you as the expert? Lots of people don't see themselves as the expert, but the moment you write that book, you are. I published a book on molestation. I didn't choose to be the face of molestation, but I understand that doors are opening for me to speak on that topic. Authors have to be prepared for that. What do you offer your target market? You have to answer the what's-in-it-for-me question. It's great that you have all these accomplishments, but what type of transformation can you get for me? The bio is not just a time to brag on accomplishments, but identify whom you serve best, why, and how.

V: That is the difference between a bio and obituary. Once you're gone, you're gone.

T: Val, the final thing many people miss in their bio is a call-to-action. For example, for booking, speaking engagements, copies of the book. Whatever it is, you need to have a line that says, "For x, here's the website, email, and phone number" (if you have a business line). The bio needs to include ways for people to contact you.

V: When I speak at events with program books, I request that they use my full professional name, Valerie J. Lewis Coleman, and include my website. Attendees have a resource to connect with me long after the event. When I'm presenting, I make an offer and do a call for emails, but I still want attendees to have information that connects to me. Website in the bio. Check!

T: That's a good point. Before you write the bio, have a website. You can send people to social media to connect with you, but you don't own those platforms. Your home is your website. You need to at least purchase the URL so you can include it in the bio. By the time you release the bio to the public, the site needs to be live so they can find out more about you.

V: Even if it's just a landing page.

T: You should also have a professional email. Create a free one. If you are going to use Gmail, make it YourName@gmail.com.

V: I have clients search <u>GoDaddy.com</u> to see if their professional name, book title, and business name are available. You had a situation where somebody wanted to add…

T: A middle initial. We were in the middle of publishing. I had to change the eBook, ISBN filing, book interior, and cover.

V: Do it right the first time.

T: Exactly.

V: It takes time and money to redo things. Some uploads require money, you have to pay the cover designer...again. The time to change the copyright, LCCN...

T: It's everywhere including the bio. At the start of the process, I ask clients how they want their name displayed. It needs to be consistent on graphics, websites, and social media.

V: Consistency is part of your branding.

T: Right. If you're going to use your middle initial, use it for all of your books.

V: Leslie Esdaile Banks wrote in multiple genres. I think we met in Detroit at Sylvia Hubbard's event. She was a seasoned professional; I was just getting started. She shared such great information. She strategically used variations of her name to represent genres. She wrote romance, sci-fi, paranormal, and a couple more genres. She used Leslie Esdaile Banks, Leslie E. Banks, LA Banks, and several other pennames by genre so her romance readers didn't pick up a paranormal novel and cringe.

T: I'm working on my first fiction piece. Depending on your many gifts, talents, or genres, your bio needs to be different. If you write in five genres, you'll probably have ten bios: long and short versions per genre. The long version should not be more than 500 words. Nobody's going to read a thousand-word bio to introduce you.

V: That's a children's book.

T: The short version should be 200 to 250 words. When you're on a radio or podcast interview, that's what the host will read.

V: You allow more words than I do. I use 250 words for the interior bio, so it fits on one page in book form and 100 words for the one on the back cover. With all the other marketing copy on the back cover, I need that real estate.

T: Don't be married to the bio. You're going to massage it to make it fit. Some online applications for speakers limit you to 150 characters.

V: Not words, characters.

T: You really have to cut it. And if it doesn't pop, they won't call you.

V: Your bio is a living document that will and should change.

T: I think the only ones that expire are ours because we're so busy working on everybody else's.

V: It takes lots of work to produce high-quality books. But I love what I do. I love empowering authors and positioning them for success. Debuting as bestsellers, selling all their books, ordering more books, getting paid speaking engagements. Dr. Townsend is my top-selling author of all time. She's had great success with TV, radio, and newspaper. I crafted her bio, book synopsis, and book title. When she came to me, the title of her book was *Take TiME*. I asked why the m and e were capital letters. "That means take time for ME." I said, "No. That looks like a typo." From a publisher/editor perspective, I was drawn to the lower case I, not the capital M E. I'm so glad she's teachable.

We talked about her process and the message she wanted to convey. As she told me her story about writing the book for busy working women, she said, "Val, I realized that it all started when I stopped using lotion." Ding! Check a winner! Chills went through me. I said, "That's the title!" *It All Started When I Stopped Using Lotion.* We added a subtitle so readers can identify and self-select: *One Woman's Journey from Chaos to Calm.*

T: People have to be flexible and willing to change their title. Authors have said to me, "The bio and cover are done." When they send it to me, most times, it's not done…right.

V: My publishing clients have one-on-one and online training to help them sell more books. During a live Q & A, Chef Keith Denard Jones said, "Val, I thought my book was finished when I sent it to you. But no, no, no."

T: Nowhere near.

V: I add, move, and remove content and research while editing manuscripts. The author and I go back and forth until the manuscript is ready for a proofreader. The final version of *Well Done: Bringing Soul to the Recipe of Life* (TheWellDoneBook.com) was such a great read, that the proofreader expressed how much she enjoyed it. For those clients who are teachable, willing to learn, and implement the things that I share, not only is it good for this book project, but it prepares them for the next one. Most of my clients have done multiple books so they can rinse and repeat the lessons learned.

T: Absolutely. Other uses for the bio are the media kit, speaker one sheet, and at the end of a media release. If you want to land speaking engagements, your bio has to be great.

V: A bionic bio that triggers a response and action. You want people to feel what you've written. Because when they know, like, and trust you, they're more inclined to connect with you, which means they're connected to your message, which means they're willing to buy your book, bring you in to speak, and hire you for whatever.

In your experience, what is the biggest writing challenge for authors and how do you serve them to overcome it?

T: Organizing their thoughts and getting them ready for publication. People have a good story; they just don't know how to put pen to paper. I help them bring their story to life. I'm working with a client whose book is on leadership. I'm asking questions to develop his message. Because if a book doesn't solve a problem, you risk people not buying it.

Some people get stuck and take ten, twenty years to finish one book. When you have guidance, it doesn't have to take that long. I published my first book with you in 2010. Now I'm up to about seventeen books.

V: Wow. And it started with one book. Now you're ghostwriting, publishing clients, and hosting events. You serve writers to break through the inability to capture their story by ghostwriting. Tell us about that.

T: Part of the ghostwriting process is understanding who they want to serve and why. Before you pay me great money to write this book, why do you want it written? Many writers believe their book is for everybody, but that's not true. You can scale better with books that are for a specific market versus a wide audience. My newest anthology, *Hush,* is specifically for women who have endured sexual abuse as adults.

V: How you tell your story, position your book, and connect with your readers are essential to ongoing success.

T: Whether clients enroll in the book coaching cohort or ghostwriting, it's about building a brand around their message. One of my clients wrote a book on the importance of African American women in leadership in Corporate America having African American women mentors. Her mentor is a White male because of the lack of African American women in corporate leadership. She received her books on Inauguration Day when the first woman vice president, Kamala Harris, was installed. The author has gotten several speaking engagements including with Jack and Jill, an organization for Black families raising Black children in predominantly White neighborhoods.

V: Good for her. One of my clients, Toni Perry Gillespie, wrote *I'm Here, Now What: A Woman's*

Guide in Corporate America. Not specifically for women of color, but women in the corporate arena. Believing that your book is for everybody is the rice-on-the-wall philosophy. I'm going to throw rice on a wall and hope something sticks. When you are clear about your ideal reader, what they need, and how you provide it for them, it's easier to connect with them. You know where they are. If you wrote a book for women of domestic or sexual abuse, you wouldn't necessarily go to Bishop TD Jakes' Manpower Conference.

T: Right. Women's shelters, YWCA, and women's ministries at churches.

V: Would you rather be a small fish in a big pond or a big fish in a small pond? Find your niche, operate in your niche. I have a literary friend who wrote a book about fibromyalgia. She was dubbed The Fibro Lady. She managed her fibromyalgia by changing her diet and lifestyle to avoid the pain that came with the condition. Her market is very niche. She connects with small groups of about twenty people. She created bundle packages with her books, supplements, and private mentoring. In a two-hour session, she can make a couple thousand dollars because she has what they want and need. If she only spoke to one group a week, her back-of-the-room sales can earn six figures.

I mentored a pastor who wrote a novel about domestic abuse. It was based on his life—his wife verbally, emotionally, and physically abused him for years. He accepted that as normal because he was abused as a child and watched his father mistreat his mother. When he sent me the book for critique, it was filled with cursing. I said, "Sir! Pastor, who is this book for?" He said that he wrote it for Christians to understand that abuse is in the church. "You can't use these words." Not to say that the saints don't cuss, but they don't want to read about your cussing in a book categorized as Christian fiction. He explained that his wife used the words…at the church. Jesus! "I appreciate that; however, you're writing this as a novel, so you can change her words. It doesn't have to be a verbatim quote. As a creative writer, you can use more appropriate words for your audience. With narrative, dialogue, and indirect dialogue, readers will understand that she was cursing without the curse words. In *The Goody Box Book*, I said, "She spewed expletives," when Deborah caught her man in bed with another woman.

T: You definitely do not want to offend your readers.

V: Right. Unless you built your brand on offending people like comedians or controversial talk show hosts.

Another thing about the bio is that it must be edited and typo free. I was at an American Library Association (<u>ALA.org</u>) Conference with Vanessa Miller Pierce. A young lady in the booth next to me wanted to swap books.

T: It's not a swap meet. We don't swap.

V: Right. I am fiscally responsible to my publisher. If I find value in your book, I will buy it, not ask you to exchange titles. To make matters worse, she had a typo in her bio on the back cover. The name of her company was incorrect. I don't remember the exact wording, but she acknowledged the error. If the name of your business on the cover is wrong, more than likely, mistakes are rampant throughout the book. No thanks.

T: I review the front cover, back cover, and spine from all angles.

V: All of that. And I have my authors do the same. It's important to send your bio and back cover copy to the editor.

T: The cover is usually done after the editorial process. Authors expect the graphic designer to edit. Whatever content you give them is what they drop.

V: Have a professional editor, not Pooky and Ray Ray, edit your content, bio, and back cover description. Also, your speaker one sheet, media releases, and any marketing elements. Wonder why you hear crickets? You sent junk and got silence in return. Last question. What is your favorite resource and why?

T: Having supported many Christian authors, the *Christian Writer's Manual of Style* is my favorite resource. Writers think that they can copy and paste the Word. They don't think about copyright infringement. They don't know how to format Scripture or cite the Bible versions on the copyright page. They don't know if it's appropriate to capitalize pronouns like he, him, or me in reference to God, Jesus, and the Holy Spirit. That resource addresses all that and more. Many Christian authors don't learn the rules because they expect the editor to know them. That book saved me lots of heartache with authors who wanted to capitalize everything. According to this style guide, that word should/should not be capitalized.

V: There are different editing styles: AP, Chicago, MLA.

T: If it's not a Christian book, I default to AP Style. The book is updated every two years. Most authors won't know the difference because it's more of a journalistic thing. If you're going to write long-term, you need to study the craft. If your plan is one-and-done, not so much.

V: The better you write it, depending upon the editor and how they charge, you can save money.

T: Save time and money.

V: If an editor charges by the hour and they don't have to do much research and correction—because you did it yourself—you save money. Plus, it makes you a better writer.

T: It does.

V: Tenita, I love you. I'm so proud of you. I am launching Pen of The Writer Academy (PenOfTheWriterAcademy.com) soon. I want you to be an expert guest speaker for my cohort.

T: Thank you.

Authors worldwide write better thanks to editorial guru and authorpreneur, Tenita C. Johnson. Perfecting manuscripts for hundreds of best-selling authors, she's on a mission to end the prominent everyday abuse of the English language and rectify punctuation pet peeves. As the founder and CEO of So It Is Written, LLC, Tenita collaborates with industry professionals to take manuscripts to the marketplace, positioning authors for success in the literary world. Well known by many as a human spell check, noun nerd, and grammar police, she proudly wears the badge of honor to correct and serve. Dubbed the editor's editor, and the book bully, she empowers aspiring authors to write from the editor's point of view to save time and money. She positions writers as experts, empowering them to create their own writing/editorial business and develop multiple streams of income. Connect with Tenita for ghostwriting, book coaching, or publishing.

<u>Connect with Tenita</u>
SoItIsWritten.net
Amzn.to/3xhXNae
Facebook.com/TenitaBestseller
LinkedIn.com/in/TenitaJohnson
Instagram.com/TenitaBestseller
Twitter.com/TenitaJEditor

<u>Tenita's Favorite Resource</u>
Christian Writer's Manual of Style by Robert Hudson

Because I Listened to My Publisher: Debuting as a Bestseller

Karen M. R. Townsend, Ph. D.

V: Joining me today is best-selling author, diversity thought leader, and women's empowerment expert, Dr. Karen M. R. Townsend. Dr. Karen hosts one of the nation's longest running women's conferences, Sister to Sister. She is a subject matter expert who speaks to national organizations, conducts international workshops and contributed to *The Shriver Report*. I met Dr. Karen over fifteen years ago, standing in line at the bank. She stood in front of me. The introvert in me slid a postcard of my upcoming writer's event on the counter. She read it and then turned around and started talking to me. Lord Jesus! But I'm glad she did. I'm so glad God put her in my life. She is a dear friend and accountability partner.

K: Valerie, thank you for inviting me to be part of this project. Our relationship began at the bank, and I needed you in my life. I had a book in me that I was trying to birth. You were my writing doula. Can I say that?

V: Yes, you can. Dr. Karen is the top-selling QueenVPublishing.com author of all times. Her book, *It All Started When I Stopped Using Lotion: One Woman's Journey from Chaos to Calm*, debuted as a bestseller. That's a big deal. You were the featured author at one of my citywide book events and in less than four hours you sold 104 books! That's amazing especially since most authors only sell 250 books for the life of a book. You sold more books than anyone of the 700 authors who signed at Dayton Book Expo.

During the expo, an author pulled me over to express his concern that you had a line of people at your table. I explained to him that you took the time to personally invite those guests. Instead of complaining about the line forming in front of him, which was several tables deep, I suggested that he use the opportunity to speak to those people who were anxiously awaiting to speak to you and tell them about his book. Get out of your seat and talk to those people. Doc, you didn't stop there. During the event, you implemented strategies to attract even more people to you and your table. I want to know what you did before the event to have a groupie line that stretched about fifty feet before social distancing.

K: I'm going to talk about what I did to prepare for that day, and things that I could have done but didn't do. Working with you, Valerie, not only did you help me finish the book, you published it, and talked to me about how to market it. Lots of self-published authors believe that if you write it, they will buy, which is not necessarily the truth. The only way you can assume that your book is going to sell is if you are someone like Michelle Obama. Everybody in the world knows her. Or Michael Jordan because he's the greatest athlete of all time, as some say, or if you are a celebrity of some sort. All they have to do is write a book, put their face on the front cover, and people are going to buy it.

I'm a first-time author and what I learned from you is nobody knows Dr. Karen Townsend. I don't need to put my face on the cover of my book because if somebody sees it at Barnes and Nobles, they don't know who I am. My face is not going to attract them to my book. But the things you told me to do I did. Like make a list of all the organizations you're a part of. Make a list of social groups that you interact with. I have three degrees, so I made a list of friends and colleagues from those universities. I reached out to the alumni associations. I am a member of Alpha Kappa Alpha Sorority, Incorporated, so I contacted my sorority sisters. I volunteer for a couple of local nonprofit organizations, so I let those organizations know I had a book. I went through my cell phone and email list to let everyone know that I was really excited about my book that was debuting at Dayton Book Expo. I invited them to attend to celebrate the release of my first book.

"You have not because you ask not." I asked individuals and partnered with organizations. As a result, people said yes to my invitation. I can't say that I thought to do that. Your tutelage and guidance led me. I listened and it paid off for me.

My favorite color is pink. The book cover has pink on it, I had on a pink dress, and I had pink roses on my table. One of the things I focused on in the book was encouraging people, especially women, to take time for themselves. The bouquet of roses had a sign that read, "Stop and smell the roses." Visuals get people to stop by the table, but the real work happened before the event.

V: What tools or mechanisms did you use to invite guests?

K: I used postcards you provided, flyers, emails, and texts. Since I'm old school, I made phone calls. Every medium that you could use, I used to reach people in my circle.

V: Whether you're going to an event as a vendor, speaker, or featured author, don't sit back and say, "I'll just show up and let the organizer do the work to market my participation." No, you made the effort to ensure that when people came, they came looking for you. And that's what I was trying to get that gentleman to understand. How many people did he invite? How many of the four or five media releases I wrote did he reshare? How many people on social media did he let know he was going to be there? Did he implement any of the bazillion marketing strategies I shared with all participating authors? Since he was from

Cincinnati and had no following in Dayton, I asked, "What did you do to connect with the people in Dayton to let them know that this author —who was well-known in Cincinnati—had come to town?" He had an oh-she-called-me-on-it look on his face.

About sixty authors participated. I'm sure that the people who came for you, supported the other authors. A byproduct of your marketing efforts was that other authors benefited. Absolutely phenomenal.

Previous authors created their own invitations and mailed them as if it were a wedding or birthday party. It's great that you put your own marketing campaign in place versus relying solely on our corporate efforts. Tell me, who came the furthest to support you?

K: One of my college friends came all the way from Phoenix, Arizona.

V: That's a good distance. Relationship attracts people to you and your message. The value of your relationship with that gentleman was such that he invested in airfare, hotel, and possibly a rental car to get your book, which is $12.95.

I don't know if he bought more than one copy, but that's a level of support you just can't get by hoping people show up.

K: And he came with a friend. That's another thing writers need to understand: your network is larger because of the people your people know. Several people came and brought friends. So, when you share your passion about your book with your circle of friends, ask them to bring a friend. You could potentially double the number of books you sell. I know Valerie who knows people I don't know. If she's excited about my book, she's likely to tell other people about it. You benefit from communicating your passion to those around you, and then encouraging them to share with others.

"To whom much is given much is required." Two of the nonprofits that I support, and will always support, are the Dayton's Boys and Girls Club and the YWCA because of the work that they do with women and girls. After the expo, I partnered with them to host book signings. I invited people and each organization invited people. For every book sold, I donated a portion of the proceeds to the respective nonprofit. You don't have to do this as a solo author. Think about who you know, think about organizations that you are affiliated with. If you have a positive relationship with those organizations, they are going to be excited about helping you promote and sell your book.

These book events started because of the success at Dayton Book Expo and the buzz about it. Valerie, it's all because of your work and commitment to authors. I wouldn't have thought about these things. I know how to do what I do. For people who have a book idea, you may need someone to support you through the process. Someone like Valerie J. Lewis Coleman can be a game changer for you.

V: Thank you, Doc. It's so true that a mentor with proven results can take you leaps and bounds toward success. You took my advice, tweaked it for your benefit, and got momentum.

And you invited your church members. An older gentleman, I believe he said that he was a deacon, strutted in to get his autographed copy.

K: And you know what else I did, Valerie? The year the book came out was my high school class reunion. I went to Kentucky and my high school helped promote a book signing at a public library.

V: That's why you are the top-selling Queen V Publishing author. You do the work. Even celebrities promote when their books release. Although they might not exert continuous momentum like self-publishers have to do, they will hit the media circuit interviewing on late night TV shows and Good Morning America. They have access to national publicity that we often don't. They do interviews to boost momentum, do their run, and then you don't hear about it anymore. As self-published authors, we have to keep that momentum going to stay relevant.

K: My husband says that I'm about semantics because I minored in English in college. I never say I am a self-published author. I say that my book was published by a small, independently-owned, female-owned publishing company.

V: I love it.

K: It's important for me to say that because I want to give props to my publisher, Queen V Publishing. There is this perception that self-published means not-as-good, lower quality, or you couldn't make it with a New York publisher. That's not my way of thinking. I was highly served by Queen V Publishing. I got care and guidance that I would have never gotten from a larger publishing company. I didn't publish it myself, Queen V Publishing did.

V: Thank you. You're absolutely right. A stigma is attached to self-publishing because so many people generate junk. Libraries, bookstores, and schools often don't want to carry their books because they weren't professionally edited or missing critical information. Some organizations won't even touch a book if they know it's been self-published. So, thank you for that admonishment. That's a good nugget for authors. As I tell my clients, there are five levels to book publishing.

Level one: I put a book out there. I did the cover myself. I read over it but didn't have it edited by professionals. I just pushed submit on Kindle and bam! I'm an author. Those authors aren't going to sell many books because they didn't invest in it. Why would you expect anyone else to buy into your project when you didn't care enough to invest?

Level two: You hired someone to design the cover and invested in one level of editing, for example proofreading, but you needed the deep-dive developmental/content editing. The book is a little better and you might sell a few more books, but you probably won't break that 250 threshold.

Level three: I work to debut my books and those of my clients at this level. These books are professionally engineered and designed to get paid speaking engagements, media attention, and book sales. Doc, your book debuted at this level. Back to your impressive marketing. *The Shriver Report* is a big deal. We're talking Maria Shriver, right?

K: Yes, Maria Shriver.

V: Media attention is a big deal. You've been in various newspapers and magazines. You won all kinds of awards, not necessarily attributed directly to the book, but the book helped boost your credibility and brand your expertise. Phenomenal.

K: Valerie, it is cool to be able to say that you are an award-winning, best-selling author. The accolades give you access to opportunities that may or may not align directly with your book. Being a published author gives you a level of credibility that people who aren't authors can't necessarily access.

V: Absolutely. Credibility and celebrity come with authorship. How have you used *It All Started When I Stopped Using Lotion,* which we dubbed *The Lotion Book,* to open other opportunities?

K: I do work around diversity, equity, and inclusion and leadership. I'm also passionate about programs for women and girls. At the beginning of the year, I make a hot list of the companies I want to work with; many of them are women-serving organizations. After an introductory email or phone call, I mail an autographed copy of my book to a key decision maker. Once that person reads the book, I often get a follow-up request to do a workshop, keynote, or presentation to women leaders. If your book is high-quality, edited properly, and well-marketed, it becomes a calling card, a business card. It's a preview of who you are and your message.

V: Absolutely. It's not just the book. If you position it well, it opens many doors. Another aspect is pricing. You don't just throw any price on there because you spent way too much to publish it.

Let's get back to the other two book levels. Level three is where the books I publish debut: professionally engineered and designed to land paid speaking engagements, media attention, and book sales.

Level four: Books that hit a national best-selling list. Seventy percent of Queen V Publishing's clients are best-sellers, and like Dr. Karen, on multiple platforms. However, level four is national bestsellers lists: *New York Times, USA Today,* NAACP Image Award. None of us have hit that mark…yet.

K: Before you can get to level five, you have to start at level three. The lower levels are where self-publishing gets the bad name. You don't know what you don't know so your book will probably hit the first two levels. Working with someone like you, Valerie, positions authors for levels four and five. You can't go from level one to level five. Some people think, "I'm going to write this book and it'll be on the *New York Times* bestseller list." No, booboo.

You haven't taken the necessary steps to ensure success. People want to do it quick, fast, and cheap, but you're not going to number five. Not to dash your dreams, but that's probably not going to happen.

V: That's reality. If you cut corners and rush the process, you get what you paid for, and money is time.

K: I don't want people to do that because then it gives my book a bad name. Because your book is poor quality, people want to look at my book with the side-eye. I did it the right way; the right way for me.

V: Absolutely. You debuted at level three. Levels four and five require intense marketing. Being a *New York Times* or *USA Today* best-selling author requires strategy, time, and money. Level five, the pinnacle for authors, is selling books into perpetuity. Dr. Seuss has been gone for years, and he's still making millions a year from book sales. JK Rowling and the Harry Potter Series. Level five is generating money on top of money long after the book released including movies, merchandising, and everything that follows. If your book debuts at level three, the rest is marketing and persistence. If you don't start at level three, you're producing junk, and junk doesn't sell well, except for Fred Sanford. Actually, I never saw him selling any junk. He never sold anything, did he?

K: No. The other thing about levels one and two, people may buy your book because you're a friend or cousin, but they probably aren't going to recommend it to others.

V: And they are not going to buy your next book.

K: What we want to do as authors, as people with messages, is get that message to as many people as possible. My dream is to speak my way around the world. While I'm working toward that dream, my book is going in front of me. It's exciting when I get notification on Amazon that someone in the United Kingdom or South Africa purchased my book. *The Lotion Book* has gone places I haven't. That only happens when you have a high-quality book that people read and tell others about.

V: Yes, word-of-mouth is the most powerful marketing tool. Social media is great for generating awareness, but a reader telling somebody, "You have to get this book. It is phenomenal. I have new tools that changed my life."

You have tools, strategies, and checklists in your book. We wanted it to be interactive and it's conversational, which I love. It's like you're talking to your girlfriend.

K: The checklist was another Valerie J. Lewis Coleman suggestion. Having checklists and reflective questions is great because readers are less likely to share the book with others. My personal thoughts, private notes, and personal assessments are in there, so you have to buy your own copy. Remember that commercial, "Can I listen to your album?" "No, my brother, you have to get your own." I recommend that every author consider putting a checklist, fill-in-the-blank, or assessment because that personalizes the book for the reader.

V: Absolutely. They get the transformation, and you get more sales because they aren't willing to share the book. In my bestselling novel, *The Forbidden Secrets of the Goody Box,* I have a reading group guide. Women take introspective reflection into why they draw the type of men they don't want, and how they can do things differently to attract and keep lasting love. It makes you dig deep, be expressive, and capture things that you haven't told anyone else. Readers tend not to share *The*

Goody Box Book. Such a great strategy. I'll take the accolades, thank you.

Back to the expo. We talked about what you did in advance. You did follow-up phone calls to confirm that people were coming, and you landed interviews. Did you get a TV interview before that event or as a result of that event?

K: I got interviews as a result of the event.

V: TV, radio, and newspaper are free publicity that keeps momentum going. You distributed postcards and posted on social media. Facebook Live was not available then, but if it was, you probably would have done some during the event. "Hey, friends. I'm here at Sinclair for Dayton Book Expo debuting my first book. I'm at table number such and such. Come get your autographed copy and self-care strategies."

The day of the event, you mentioned your professional attire. You will not believe the number of people I have seen at book events who look like they just got out of bed. I get that you want to be comfortable, especially if you're there at an all-day event, but there needs to be a level of professionalism. You can be professional and comfortable so that you project a powerful brand image. Especially if your book is nonfiction and you're looking to land speaking engagements and connect with influencers.

The day of the event, didn't you text people to remind them on the event and where you were in the Great Hall?

K: Absolutely. I also had a team there to support me. My team sent text messages and made phone calls. "Don't forget Dr. Karen is at the Dayton Book Expo today. Come by." Once again, not just my personal network, but the network of people around me. I also had people at my table to process transactions.

V: You had a long line. You needed help with that.

K: To get everyone's name spelled correctly — something else you taught me, Valerie — I had Post-it Notes for guests to write their name. When it came time for me to sign their book, I didn't have to ask, "Is that Valerie with a y, ee, or ie?" It was printed on the note, so I greeted them, personalized the autograph with their name, and kept the line moving.

V: That's great, especially when you're in a big, loud space. Trying to understand what they were saying, would have slowed your process.

About your staff. Your executive assistant is assisting you today. She's wonderful. Shout out to Syron! When you left your table to speak, you didn't have to stop transacting business. You had people to transact business on your behalf and collect emails. It's important for authors to understand that when you go to multi-day or long-hour events, you don't want to do that alone.

K: No. And if for some reason you don't have someone who can staff your table while you step away to conduct a workshop, speak, or use the restroom, another Valerie J. Lewis Coleman tip, cover your table. If you have organza material to cover your table, people can still see the products. However, the covering indicates that they can't pick up a book for free. That happens doesn't it, Valerie?

V: It happens. I volunteered at your Sister to Sister Conference. I saw a lady grab a book from your product table. I said, "Excuse me." She said, "I thought it was free." "No, it's not free. Would you like to purchase a copy?" People have done that to me, too. That's one reason I track my starting inventory. I only put so many books on the table for the appearance of scarcity, but it's also easier to see if anything is missing at a glance.

K: This is what I do, Valerie. I have books that I'm not going to sell. Maybe it's damaged or I made a mistake while autographing, but I put those books on display. Hopefully, no one will take them without paying, but if they do, I won't feel bad because it's not a book that I wanted to sell. When people say, "I'd like to purchase it." I say, "Let me get you a fresh, untouched copy." They feel special. So rather than putting your good, saleable product on display, if you have damaged books that you're not going to sell, put those on the table.

V: Good point. I use easels or plate stands to display each title. I wrote display on the outer edges of the book because the pages are frayed, or covers are bent back from people reviewing them. I'm not losing inventory every time someone flips through the book. The display book and easel are on top of the inventory that I want to sell. It's kind of a safeguard to keep the other books from getting touched.

Pink is your favorite color and you're an AKA. Did you become an AKA because pink is your favorite color or did pink become your favorite color because you're an AKA?

K: It's a confounding variable. Pink has been my favorite color since third grade. When I went for a college visit, I met nice young ladies who wore pink jackets. I loved the jacket and wanted to join the "club" when I got on campus. I didn't know anything about sororities. It worked out for me that AKAs wore pink and green and pink is my favorite color.

V: I incorporate clients' favorite colors on covers.

K: Since pink is my favorite color and AKA colors are pink and green, it was an easy choice. When I'm doing events, the colors pop. Any time an AKA stops by, they ask if I'm in the sorority. A subtle marketing tactic.

V: Pink is the "universal color" for women and your book is for women, we pulled in that element, too. Another tactic we used for your cover was the white space, which helps it stand out amongst other books on a shelf or table display. And of course, the woman's feet. Give a brief summary about your book? Because those feet are a mess. Somebody asked me, "Are those Dr. Karen's feet?"

K: No, I outsourced that job to a foot model. In *It All Started When I Stopped Using Lotion: One Woman's Journey from Chaos to Calm*, lotion is a metaphor for the little things we do for ourselves. And at one point, I stopped doing the little things. What I discovered was when you stop doing one thing, it's easy to stop doing another, and another, and another. For me, it was lotion. I love bubble baths. One day, I was in a hurry, so after the bubble bath, I did not put on lotion. The next day, not only did I skip the lotion, I also skipped the bath. I did take a shower, Valerie, in case you were wondering.

V: Very important to note.

K: It was fall when you wear more clothes. I stopped shaving my legs, stopped shaving my underarms. Why waste that time when nobody's going to see them anyway? Over a series of weeks, I stopped doing more and more things for me. During a spa day with my girlfriends, the last service was a pedicure. The nail tech said, "You have a callus on the bottom of your foot. Do you walk a lot?" I said, "Yes, but I've always walked a lot." "Do you wear heels?" "I wear heels every day." "When you take a bath, do you use a pumice stone?" "When I take a bath?" I rewound my life over the last few weeks and couldn't remember when I had taken a bath. I had become a stressed, angry, impatient person and I realized that it all started when I stopped using lotion. I want my readers to understand that it's okay to make yourself a priority and that self-care is not selfish.

V: Not at all. Like flight attendants say, "In the event of an emergency, put on your oxygen mask first." Let's get back to the day of the event. You had professional attire, you texted reminders to people, and you had a team. After you autographed the book, you took pictures with readers for credibility and celebrity. "I'm with the author" and "I know Dr. Karen Townsend, who earned a Ph.D." We didn't preface your name with Dr., but we put Ph.D. after it. Not self-proclaimed or honorary. You earned that advanced degree which is another boost of credibility.

Your table had bright colors and a sign indicating the retail price. You had organza, rose petals, and you collected emails. What was your strategy for collecting emails?

K: I asked people to provide their email for an opportunity to win a prize. I had a bundle, which was an autographed copy of the book, a bottle of lotion, and other self-care goodies. Another thing I had on my table was a bottle of lotion. I encouraged people to use it as a simple act of self-care, which is the message of the book. All those things engage your potential buyers. It's not just

"Buy my book, give me your money." Sensory things took place. Stop and smell the roses. Put on scented lotion. Win a prize. It was visually stimulating and kinesthetic to engage readers. They're not just buying your book. They're having an experience and that's what people remember.

V: I remember your results so well that I made it part of my event checklist for authors. The average sale at a signing is seven books. I don't recall where I got that statistic, but that means some authors sell a couple books, while authors like you sell 104. This sales continuum makes a difference when you have your individual marketing campaign to get people there.

Another thing that helped to solidify your book sales was your personality and nonverbal communication. You stood to speak with guests. Many authors sit behind the table, which is a barrier to communication, whereas you stood in front of or beside your table to connect with them.

You took advantage of the opportunity to speak. If I don't have an opportunity to speak, I'm not interested in sitting at a table hoping people come to me. I prefer to speak so people can engage with me. Even though you had a plethora of people coming to see you, those who didn't know you were intrigued by the line. When I announced that Dr. Karen was speaking about her book in the auditorium, people who didn't know you came to listen. People tend to invest in those they know, like, and trust, and your dynamic presentation made your groupie line even longer. I'm sure the across-the-aisle author was quite perturbed, but he didn't request to speak, an opportunity available to all participating authors.

K: Even with a speaking platform, some people only speak. I encourage authors to engage the audience as part of the presentation. Invite them to talk to you and ask questions. Encourage them to jot answers. One of the chapters in my book is about joy. As I spoke on the big stage, I asked people, "What brings you joy? Make a list of things that bring you joy." I pulled them into my presentation by having them recall and write. The second question: When was the last time you did that? I asked audience members for feedback. One woman raised her hand. When I asked her what brings her joy, she said "Dancing. I love to dance." I said "That sounds great. When was the last time you went dancing?" She said that it had been ten years. She hadn't been dancing in a decade! I told the audience, "We can't put those things that bring us joy on hold for ten years. We have to make ourselves a priority. We have to start putting on lotion." By involving the audience, I drove home a point. Somebody in the audience needed the lesson of the book. Guess what. People who hadn't done joyous things for two years said that they didn't want to wait. Following my session, the dance lady and other audience members bought the book. Don't just speak to your audience. Engaging your audience is key.

V: Yeah, you make everything into a workshop. It's a great skill I admire in you. You added new contacts to your email list. What do you do to stay in touch with them?

K: I am working on automating this process, but I'm more hands-on and I need to better understand the technology. On a regular basis, I send messages to my list. I do something called "Happy Friday" where I send words of inspiration and motivation to stay in contact. It serves two purposes. When my next book is ready for release, they already know me instead of who is this person trying to sell me something?

The second thing: Even if they don't need the services I provide right now, they see my name on a regular basis. When they do need my services, it's a no brainer.

V: You are "top of mind" as Darnyelle says. You're the first person they think of when they need help with diversity and inclusion, women empowerment, or leadership. That's kind of how you landed *The Shriver Report*.

K: Another reason to have a book is because you can repurpose the information in it. Your book may be seven, ten, or fifty chapters. Each chapter can be a speaking engagement, podcast episode, or an article. In a conversation with a friend, she said, "You should do something bold today." I said,

"Okay. What?" She said, "I don't know. I don't care. Just do something bold." I received *The Shriver Report*, an international online magazine focused on issues important to women and girls, which is important to me. The digital newsletter had a button at the bottom of the page for contributing writers. I clicked on it and landed at a brief questionnaire. I got an immediate response requesting more about my ideas. I wrote about a paragraph, sent my pitch, and got an auto responder. "Thank you for your submission. We get hundreds a day. If there's an interest, we'll be in touch."

About two weeks later, I got an email from one of the editors apologizing for the delay. She had been off sick. She expressed interest in my idea and asked if I could submit an article in two weeks. Absolutely! I had an article published by Maria Shriver, the former wife of Arnold Schwarzenegger, the Terminator. It is one of my proudest moments. I realized that I was not effectively monitoring social media because unbeknownst to me, the article was posted on Twitter. My article was exposed to many people, and I didn't fully leverage that opportunity.

That's something else for authors: make sure that your social media game is tight. Social media allows you to meet people you couldn't meet under normal circumstances. I looked back on that missed opportunity, but I gave myself grace. It was a learning opportunity.

V: Going forward, you can use Google alerts <u>Google.com/alerts</u> for notification of online activity. Use your name, book title, and anything else that pertains to you. When somebody publishes something on the internet about you, you get notification. Every now and then, do a Google search of your name, your book title, and business in quotation marks to see your reach.

I did that recently and found that my information is on *Washington Post*'s site. One of my stepfamily quotes on <u>GoodReads.com</u> was captured in an article. Keanu Reeves, yes, Neo from *The Matrix*, retweeted one of my posts. It was one of his relationship quotes. I assume he got a Google alert because he's not one of my Facebook friends. I grabbed the screen shot for bragging rights.

We talked about what you did for the event. What things did you not do?

K: I didn't do it for the event or the book. I did a presentation titled, *If Only I had Listened to My Publisher: Strategies to Market Your Book before It's Published.* It was filled with things I learned from you, Valerie. We talked about a number of them, but one really cool idea I wish I had done was release a teaser or sample chapter. And think of it like this, before Janet Jackson releases an album, she releases a single. All spring long, you're listening to that one song. You're bopping to the music and cannot wait for the album to drop months later. Authors can do the same thing with their book. Pique interest so they ask, "When is your book coming out?" As soon as the book drops, they want to buy it because they've been waiting for it.

V: Create a swell. Build momentum in advance of your release.

K: I have my own inventory of books. You can buy my book on Barnes and Nobles, Amazon, and other online marketplaces. After I published my book, I understood why new musicians sold CDs out of the trunk of their car. Because when you sell direct to consumer, you get all the money.

When Warner Brothers sells your CD, they take a cut, which is the same with Amazon, Barnes and Nobles, whomever. If you have a speaking event for 5,000 people, it's challenging to pack up and sell 5,000 books. Yes, send people to Amazon. But if you have a speaking engagement in your local community, take and sell your books. When people contact me via my website or email and ask how to get my book, I encourage them to buy it from me. So as not to appear greedy or opportunistic, which I'm not, I explain that buying a book from me, allows me to autograph and personalize it with their name. Every opportunity you have to sell books direct to the consumer, do it.

V: Absolutely. That's how the reader benefits. For the author, you have a higher profit margin because you're not splitting with the distributor. You collect emails so you can stay in touch with them, which is major, especially if you're doing events or have other offers. Something I learned with my full-color children's book is that the quality of offset printers is much better and about half the cost compared to the automated digital printer used by online platforms. There are numerous reasons to send people to your website. Let's talk about your Michelle Obama experience.

K: I love Michelle Obama. My birthday is in January, her birthday is in January. So, I mailed a copy of my book to the White House for her birthday.

I didn't hear anything. I wondered if she got the book. As I arrived at the venue for an event, my phone rang. It was an unknown number, which I don't usually answer, but on this day, I answered. After I greeted the caller, the person on the other end said, "Please hold for a call from the White House." After a brief pause, with my mind racing, someone came on the line. "Hello. This is Andrew from the office of First Lady Michelle Obama. I'm calling to let you know that she received your gift. She appreciates you thinking of her on her birthday." I thanked him and then ended the call. I got a call from the White House! Fabulous! I was excited that I got the phone call, but it would really have been nice to have a thank-you note from her.

V: Receipt. Documented proof.

K: I traveled quite a bit around that time. I go to my post office box once a week, but during this period, I had not been in two weeks. When I checked my mail, it had a brown slip that notifies you of a package. The return address was the White House. "Oh, my gosh. Michelle sent me something!" I took the slip to the postmaster. She said, "I'm sorry. We returned it because it had been here too long." I went to my car devastated. I called my husband to tell him what happened. In so many words, he said, "Oh, well. That's too bad." Not what I needed to hear. Then I called my publisher and friend, Valerie J. Lewis Coleman. After I explained what happened, you said, "Call the White House." I was like, "What?" "Call the White House." "I can't call the White House." "Why not?" "Okay, okay." I called the White House and asked for the Office of the First Lady. Do you know what they said, Valerie?

V: What did they say?

K: "Which office? Do you want her social office, legislative office, or…?" "I think I want the social office." They connected me and I explained the situation. He said, "Hold on for a moment. "Yes, I can see that we sent you a package and it came back. Because of security, it has to go back through the process but let me see if we can send it again. If you don't hear from me in two weeks, call me back." He gave me his name and number. In about seven days, I received a letter from First Lady Michelle Obama. She thanked me for the copy of my book and remembering her on her birthday.

V: Like you said, "You have not because you ask not." What's the worst that could have happened?

K: Right. But it wouldn't have happened, if I didn't have *The Lotion Book* to send to her.

V: Phenomenal. In your experience, what is the biggest marketing challenge for authors?

K: Coming to grips with the fact that you have to do the work. You can't just say, "Hey, I published a book." How many books are published in a year, Valerie?

V: I don't know, but there's over 32 million books on Amazon right now.

K: It's not enough to say that you published a book. The biggest challenge is developing and implementing a solid marketing plan. The advantage I had was working with you. I'm not a book marketer, that's not my area of expertise. I leaned on you for marketing strategies. When I came up with an idea, I ran it past you to discuss the logistics and whether it made sense. People who don't do marketing, don't know how to market. I have a Ph.D., but it's not in marketing. I go to the expert who knows how to do that. That's what I think is the biggest challenge: not knowing what to do and being unwilling to ask for help.

V: And spending lots of time, energy, effort, and money doing it the wrong way. This anthology is all about doing it the right way. Last question, what is your favorite resource and why? It could be an app, service provider, website, or book.

K: Since you said app, Spotify.com. Not only does it provide music, I can listen to podcasts for motivation and inspiration.

V: Thank you so much. You have been a wealth of knowledge. She's doing big things.

K: I'm going to Google myself at your suggestion. I would love to connect with your readers to see if I can assist them. Through my company, K Townsend Consulting, we work with leaders to create inclusive environments and build strong teams. I want professionals to be able to live and lead competently.

V: Oh, yes. Confidential Conversations, Sister to Sister Conference, private and group mentoring. You have all kinds of options for leaders, experts, and authors. Dr. Karen, thank you so, so much.

Whether delivering presentations to corporate executives, or encouraging busy women to make themselves a priority, Karen M.R. Townsend, Ph.D. is an inspiring speaker. As president of KTownsend Consulting, Dr. Karen works with leaders to create inclusive environments and build strong teams to meet the needs of diverse clients. Dr. Karen is on a mission to empower one million women and girls. For three decades, she has hosted the annual Sister to Sister Conference which has been recognized as one of the longest-running women's events in the United States. Dr. Karen's first book was inspired by her own quest to find life balance. *It All Started When I Stopped Using Lotion: One Woman's Journey from Chaos to Calm* encourages women to "take their TiME: Time for ME!" Organizations across the globe use *The Lotion Book* to support the professional development of high-potential women leaders.

<u>Connect with Dr. Karen</u>
KTownsend.com
Amazon.com/Karen-MR-
Townsend/e/B00Q3G33EK
Facebook.com/Karen.M.Townsend.94
LinkedIn.com/in/dr-karen-m-r-townsend-096836
Instagram.com/KTownsend
Twitter.com/KTownsend

<u>Dr. Karen's Favorite Resource</u>
<u>Spotify.com</u> because it provides music and podcasts for motivation and inspiration.

Before You Publish: Everything You Need in Your Author Arsenal to Get Publicity

Pam Perry

V: Joining me today is awarding-winning, communications professional, author, and magazine publisher, Pam Perry. Pam is responsible for mentoring authors, speakers, and entrepreneurs to build platforms that attract major media and publishers. *Publisher's Weekly* dubbed her a PR Guru, and she is gifted in connecting the right people to the right project at the right time. I first met Pam, doing what she does, at the Christian Retailers Association Expo in Atlanta, 2007. As an introvert, I wasn't trying to talk to anyone, but Pam was not having that.

Since then, Pam spoke at my conference, Pen to Paper Literary Symposium, and we shared the stage at several Detroit events: Motown Writers and Anointed Pens.

Pam, for those who don't know you, share who you are and what you do.

P: I am a publicist by trade. That's why, in 2000, I started Ministry Marketing Solutions, Inc. to help churches and pastors market better. I left corporate as the director of public relations after about seven years. After I got married, I wanted to start a company working primarily for a niche of African American Christian authors, speakers, pastors, and churches. I didn't know how it was going to look because I didn't know anybody who had done it. I knew that I wanted to work from home using my skills in media to help ministers. The internet was fairly new and a pricey option for small business owners, so lots of people didn't have websites.

V: Social media, none of that.

P: None of it. The vision was there, but I didn't have any of the stuff to do it. I met my first client in an elevator. We struck up a conversation and he asked me what I did. When I told him PR for Christians, he said, "That's funny. I need someone to do PR for my gospel play." It happened like ta-da! I believe that was God saying, "You're on the right track."

I did PR for him, and he got front page coverage on *The Free Press*. *Perilous Times* sold out every night. He introduced me to other pastors, and it grew from there. I worked with the bishop of Greater Grace doing PR for his first book. I worked with the communications department of Word of Faith. I wrote newspaper articles for Strait Gate. When the internet caught on, I worked with more pastors and authors.

People were writing books, but they didn't know how to promote them. I had monthly face-to-face mini conferences. I pulled together information to share and they produced books. Kim Brooks was one of those people.

V: You're a public relations (PR) expert. I understand there's a difference between a publicist and a PR person.

P: People interchange a publicist and a PR person because publicists practice public relations. Publicity is what a publicist generates from a public relations campaign. It's connecting with media. When you have something written in a newspaper, interview on radio or podcast, a magazine article—online or offline—that's publicity. That's when you share your story and info with a journalist who prints or broadcasts it. It's a third-party endorsement. At times, it's hard to do because people don't know the journalists or how to approach them. They hire a publicist to pitch them to the media. A publicist's primary purpose is to book media interviews and coach you on how to leverage them.

V: The connection you provide is putting experts with reporters and others who need their expertise and content.

P: Exactly. Many people don't understand that publicity is positioning yourself for how you want people to perceive you. It goes in line with your brand and how you carry yourself.

V: Right. You can't do booty shots on your Facebook profile page and then have a fan page talking about singing for Jesus. It doesn't work like that because it's interconnected. What is the main difference between publicity and marketing?

P: Publicity is one spoke in the wheel of marketing, which includes direct mail, speaking engagements, putting a sign on the side of your car, wearing a branded t-shirt. Internet marketing, email marketing, and more. Publicity is the spoke specific to media outreach including blogs and podcasts.

V: You start with getting media attention, but as the momentum builds and opportunities come, I'm sure your clients reach out to you for help preparing for interviews.

P: Yes. That's media coaching. We help them with how to do short sound bites. I've seen pastors who don't know how to stop.

V: The third and final benediction.

P: Yes. They know how to do one-way conversations like they're used to at church, but they don't know how to dialogue during an interview. We coach them on media sound bites and more. For interviews on a national TV station, you only have two minutes; maybe ten minutes if it's local.

You can't talk too long and not have time for Q & A. You need media training to know how to speak to the media and not speak with Christianese, which is colloquial words that the church uses. You want to sound like the audience. If you're on

TBN or The Word Network, that's fine. But if you're on a news station, you want to sound like the majority of the people in the news audience. "Oh, bless the Lord. I'm highly favored," sounds weird to them.

V: And you can lose some people.

P: Yes. Take out the colloquialism.

V: Take off the bishop's garb. You mentioned sound bites which is something I talk to my clients about. With Twitter, you have 280 characters to get out your message. Please define a soundbite and how you prepare your clients to use them.

P: The first part is your message. What main thing do you want to get across? Think about a political campaign. The candidate has talking points that they want to make sure people know. The same is true for authors. If nothing else, let the audience know what the book is about, why you wrote it, and where they can get it. Sometimes the interview ends and people don't know where to get the book or connect with you.

You want to write your message in responses no more than two or three minutes. Two minutes is a long time, especially if you're doing a fifteen-minute interview. You want to deliver short, punchy things about the book so people say, "Ooh, that sounds good." Les Brown is really good at doing that. He says poetic catchy phrases. Making sure that people know how to do that starts by writing their messaging at the very beginning.

V: Absolutely. Novels require a certain word count, but you have a limited amount of time...and words for interviews. You have to condense your message. If you have a powerful sound bite, people will remember what you said long after the interview. You planted the seed. "One plants, one waters, God gives the increase." Those soundbites can be powerful tools that help your readers or audience remember who you are and what you have to say.

P: Look at TikTok or any social media platform. The attention span is much shorter. Brevity is the new currency. You want to be as brief and impactful as you can.

V: Absolutely. So, publicity is connection to media and marketing is all the other stuff in that wheel. It costs to have a publicist or PR person. Advertisement and other aspects of marketing have fees attached. Getting the word out about your book is not only about social media.

P: No, it's not.

V: I get inbox messages from people I don't know. "My book is out. Will you buy my book?" First of all, I don't know you. Secondly, I don't know if I want your book. Thirdly, we have no relationship.

P: Right. That's why I launched the Brand Accelerator Program. First, you build a platform, you build a brand, and then you get PR. People are so hung up about writing content for social media, but that's like speaking about yourself all day long and no one else vouches for you. You need to share other things like a review in *Publisher's Weekly*, a morning show interview, or podcast. That way you're spreading beyond social media. The purpose for social media is to build relationships. As people are attracted to you, they go to your website, and then you nurture that relationship. If the relationship is only on social media, it's only going to be chit-chat.

But when you go to someone's email, you're having a real discussion and you can talk further. People claim to make money on social media, but I think they added fans to their email list and marketed to them there. No one sees a tweet and says, "I want to buy that." They typically follow "the expert," watch them, maybe join their email lists, and look at other offerings. People put too much emphasis on social media, especially Instagram. Baby boomers probably can't compete with millennials on Instagram because it's a visual tool.

You're sixty years old with more experience. You could talk for an hour with in-depth knowledge or write a 500-word newspaper article as commentary. Since you have different skills, the appeal is different compared to Instagram.

V: I have 5,000 Facebook friends another couple thousand following, and a few thousand in my groups. The algorithm is such that only about five percent of your friends see your posts and it's typically the same five percent. You can put a bunch of stuff out there, but only 250 of your 5,000 friends have the ability to see it. TV, newspaper, and radio platforms tend to have a wide audience. A newspaper article, which I got for free, landed in our local newspaper. It's print circulation was 300,000, and they put it online.

P: There you go. You can be found on Google, which has more credibility than Facebook posts.

V: I'm protective of my Facebook page. People have tried to connect with my fans by posting a buy-my-book message on my page. I don't know you, I haven't read your book, and you're not about to use me as a credibility endorsement. Delete.

P: It's about etiquette when you tag someone and post on their page. You don't tag random people.

V: I ask permission. Sylvia Hubbard oversees the Motown Writers Facebook group. I'm in the group because we have spoken at each other's events. Before I posted the call-for-submissions for this anthology, I asked permission. If she had said no, I wouldn't have been mad. You don't just walk into somebody's house and sit for dinner. It doesn't work like that.

P: Nope. That's public relations: how you relate to the public. I find that when most people do their content calendar, they focus solely on social media. But the same headlines used for social media can be used as media pitches. Think of it as a pitch to your local newspaper. People think, I'm going to do my book and social media, then I want to get national attention. You start local, regional, and then national. You don't start from Facebook and go national. Many people are unaware of the process and become impatient because it takes time.

V: I worked with gospel music artists for about five years. One group said, "We want to be national." I told them, "National is just pockets of local. How about we get to the point where fans shriek for your autograph in the local mall and then swell like a pebble tossed in a pond." You can't be on the local news today and expect Good Morning America the next day. It's a process that requires lots of work.

P: It is. Some of my clients have gone national. Often, the relationship with the reporter and publicist make it happen. I got Juanita Rasmus, pastor to Beyoncé and the Knowles family, on CNN. She wasn't just another pastor because Beyoncé's name carries weight.

She had local credibility as the pastor of a mega church in Houston. She officiated Beyoncé and Jay Z's wedding and had media contacts. When she relocated to Indianapolis, I pitched her to local media. Because she wasn't as well known in Indianapolis, it was a bit harder. I lead with something that might interest them: a link to her Ted Talk, which was about her book, and an amazing electronic press kit (EPK). I noted that she was with a national publisher and included an endorsement from Tina Knowles. Buttering them up to show why they should pay attention. She was in *Psychology Today* and *Christianity Today*. Those things matter. She got on CNN because it snowballed.

V: The other thing about being on a national platform is the producers need to see you in action to know that you're not going to be a "deer in the headlights" when the camera is on.

Because if you're not familiar with interviews, studio sets, and practiced your sound bites, you don't have time to stutter, stammer, and look away from the camera. I'm sure you communicate what you should and should not wear on TV for your clients as well.

P: Definitely. That is all part of branding. One client, Nicole, was on CNBC. The producer had pitched her for one thing, but they couldn't use it. The producer asked if I had someone for another segment, and I said, "Yes, I do." I sent the link, her EPK with a background reel, and spun her expertise to fit CNBC. Why did it work? Because she was ready. When they asked about sending someone to her — in-studio interviews were avoided due to COVID — I told them that she had a studio and clenched the deal. She was an easy win. They called Tuesday; she was on air Thursday.

V: They're looking for an easy win because there's so much noise in the market. I have turned away publishing clients because they weren't teachable. Working with them was too much extra work and not worth the stress. The same thing applies to getting media attention. They're going to work with those people who are easiest, ready, and knowledgeable. So, you got some local exposure. Don't go in the studio like you're a diva.

P: Yes. That's another thing people don't realize about publicity. Pre-COVID, they wanted to do a national PR tour and asked, "Will they fly me in?" Unless you're a celebrity, travel, meals, and lodging are at your expense. Whenever you see someone on a national platform, they were in town or they flew in themselves. Now it's different because you can do Zoom interviews. Clients ask about bookstore tours, but there's not many independent bookstores. So where are you going to go? Zoom.

V: You're spending money for travel, lodging, and the bookstore fee. Are you really sure that's what you want to do?

P: You're probably selling twenty or thirty books on a good day.

V: Without having an understanding of average book sales, authors can have a grandiose expectation. When it doesn't manifest, they get frustrated. I've been to book events where I paid booth fee, hotel, meals, and lodging and sold ten books.

Considering the cost of book printing, I was in the hole. I participated in a book fair for authors of books for children of color. Because I didn't see much online marketing, I assumed attendance would be low, so I brought a client's manuscript to edit. The booth fee wasn't that expensive, and the event was a two-hour drive, so I avoided hotel fees. Other than my time, I didn't have much money invested.

About a half an hour before the event to a half an hour after, I was on my feet selling. I stopped for ten minutes to use the restroom and eat. I didn't bring anybody with me because I didn't expect much traffic. I sold forty-nine books, plus merchandise in five hours!

P: The host went for a niche audience. The more niched an author is, the better. I'm a mother of a Black child, I want to find everything I can for my child. They're reading specialized magazines like *Black Child Today* and see an ad about the book fair. If it's what they want, they will show up. They're talking to each other, so the buzz came because that's a niche.

If you can refine to a small niche, at least starting out, you'll have much more success.

V: It's better to be the big fish in a little pond, than a little fish in a big pond. Part of my training with clients is asking, "Who's the ideal reader for your book? And don't tell me everybody." How do you reach everybody? How does your message hit everybody? Everybody doesn't read. Everybody doesn't have access to books. Everybody doesn't want your book. You have to hone your ideal reader to that niche and then work it.

What three things do authors need to have in place to get solid publicity?

P: Ooh, that's good. The main thing is the platform. Who's listening to you for the message you provide? Think about someone who was Miss America. What is the thing that people know she talks about? She's going to talk about her passion, for example childhood leukemia, no matter where she goes. The people attracted to your platform get on your email list because they want more information from you. If they like what you provide, they'll share your information, which helps build your platform.

Some authors are publishing what I call vanity books. It doesn't have a platform because they're just telling their story. I explain that it needs to be a message that's going to benefit someone. It can't just be cathartic for the author to tell his/her story. What's the platform? Is it overcoming domestic violence? Sexual abuse? Drug addiction? Once you identify the message for readers, you can connect with them and collaborate with people on that platform.

Stanice Anderson was featured on CBN for her book, *I Say a Prayer for Me*. Before that, she spoke at drug rehabs and facilities that inspired people coming out of years of drug addiction. That was her platform. For years, she built her platform so that people understood what she did. The platform is number one.

After the platform, you build your brand with brand assets like a website, photos, signage, and your logo. Anything visual are branding assets that people can use to recognize you. Much of my brand is pink and my brand assets tend to have a feminine look. You're building your brand assets based on the platform, public relations, and the people who are attracted to you. So, if it's mostly men, pink should not be your primary color.

The next thing is having your digital game together. You have your platform, honing your message, and gathering people who are listening to it. You have brand assets, which could include a book trailer. Across the board, the digital game pulls it all. Your website, search engine optimization, your social media is consistent. Your bio and author photo are the same so people can recognize you across the internet. When they Google you, they'll find the same name and picture everywhere, especially when you're just starting.

I change my picture often, but since I've been doing this for over twenty years, people recognize me. I suggest using the same photo for five years, so people get to know you. Don't change it every week having people wondering if it's the same person. Those are the three things: have a platform, build your brand with brand assets, and get your digital game on point.

V: The platform is something that you're passionate about, not something just to chase the money.

P: Right. If an event organizer says, "I'll be back in five minutes. Valerie is here." Next thing you know, people are swarmed around you because you're talking about publishing. That's your platform.

It doesn't matter where you're going, you're going to talk in that direction. For me, it's PR. It's your main thing. People who write memoirs may be confused about that. "I don't have a platform. It's just my story." Even if you write fiction, you have a platform. Certain things about your novel, why you wrote the memoir, what is it that you want to share?

Many fiction authors have similar goals that they want to portray in their works. It's funny because they say, "I don't have a platform." Yes, you do. Stacy Hopkins Adams, Kim Brooks, and other novelists want to leave readers with a feeling or reaction. If they're having a conversation with someone who hasn't read the book or interviewing on a radio station, they talk about the theme and ideas from the book, their platform.

V: Right. Vanessa Miller Pierce is a Christian fiction author who also writes romance. All of her books have an underlying theme about God, forgiveness, peace, love. Virtues that may not be found in other genres. Absolutely have a platform that focuses on your passion. Elaborate for me on the digital game. Are you referring to digital downloads or eBooks?

P: Across the internet. So, if I were to Google your name, I need to see that same name everywhere.

V: Consistency.

P: My digital imprint is Pam Perry PR across everything, unless it wasn't available. The bios are basically the same. One is a micro version, one is a mini, one is a longer, but they're basically the same all the way across. If I go to your YouTube channel, I see the same banner that is on LinkedIn. It's sized different based on platform parameters, but the banner is the same. So, you have the same branding all the way across so that you're not looking scattered. Is this the same person?

V: If you confuse your intended audience, they're not going to buy from you. My brand color is purple and almost everything I put out has some purple. Being findable makes it easier for people. I can't tell you how many times I worked with authors and couldn't find their book on Amazon. The title was generic and their name common, so searching on Amazon yielded pages of results. I'm only going through the first four or five pages.

P: Right. Some people only do one page. If they don't see it on the first page, they're on to something else.

V: You have to think about all of that. If I can't find your book to prepare for a discovery call, then your readers can't find it either. That's not good. That's why I use Valerie J. Lewis Coleman as my professional name. It differentiates me from the bazillion Valerie Colemans in the world.

P: I tell clients to follow media on social media to develop a virtual relationship with them. You know what they're tweeting and doing. If you follow a newspaper, the home page will probably show some of the reporters. I read the bios to see what topics they cover. Find media specific to your topic and develop a warm relationship with them. Some media will ask for experts for a project. You can jump in, answer their questions, and assist. Even if it's not for your book right now, you're helping out a reporter and building that relationship. You can do that without subscribing to <u>HelpAReporter.com</u>. Find the media in your area and assist them.

V: Absolutely. I've gotten lots of local attention and developed relationships with some reporters. I have landed front-page, above-the-crease, full-color spots in the local Black-owned newspaper. "You have not because you ask not." Reporters are not going to automatically pick you up, so media releases are valuable tools. I have a professional relationship with a salesman at the radio station. When I invest in radio spots for my events, he opens doors for me to have interviews on these platforms. That's a free add-on for investing and it's all interconnected.

P: You can start by placing ads with them. The salesperson will introduce you to a show producer or host. It's like pay to play. They're in business and will give favor to people who invest in them. I'm so glad you mentioned the Black press. Many Black authors think that the end all be all is CNN or White publications. You will find the most love, respect, and value from your Black press. You frame your full-color article from the local Black press.

I often hear authors say, "I appreciate the NAACP Image Award the most because it came from my own." You can join NNPA.org, a trade association of over 200 African American community newspapers. Visit Black News USA at BlackNews.com to find Black newspapers. Most major cities have at least one Black-owned and operated newspaper. Consider online papers like MadameNoire.com, TheGrio.com, TheRoot.com, Blavity.com. You will find lots of Black media, not The Shade Room, that you can approach as an African American. You have something in common so pitch it. See what else they need and offer to help.

V: It's a reciprocal relationship. They need content to keep momentum, keep their audience intrigued, and for advertising dollars, while you need to get out your message. If they do digital and print, the circulation can be significant.

P: Yes. Media begets media. A young lady pitched me for my podcast, *Get Out There and Get Known*. Typically, I only interview media people or PR colleagues, but this young lady had such an interesting pitch. She sent an email asking how I selected guests for the podcast. She included a link to a Jamaican newspaper article about her and her new book, *What are You Good at?* The article was so interesting and flattering that I brought her on the podcast. After the show aired, she wrote me a letter explaining that she got two invitations to speak and a guest feature on a webinar.

Although she lived in Miami, that Jamaican newspaper had an affinity for her as a native islander. Whatever the circulation, they ran a full article and she repurposed it to land interviews. When I asked how she got the write up, she said, "I'm from Jamaica, so I just called the editor."

V: Good for her. It's a no brainer.

P: Yes. The lowest hanging fruit is usually the places you visit the most. You probably spent a hundred thousand dollars at your college, so contact the alumni newsletter. Even if you're not an alumnus, they need content for every publication. Whatever coverage you get, share it on your website and social media. I tell people to look at your lowest hanging fruit, before trying to reach Oprah and CNN.

V: Where you have affiliations—relationships— makes sense. High school, college, your church, where you conduct business...

P: Sorority.

V: Sorority. I was working to get momentum for my children's book, *Oh, The Things I Can Be When I See Me* (ThingsICanBe.com). Someone posted a picture of the book and commented, "I got my book, Val. Thank you so much." The church administrator saw it and commented, "Wait a minute! You have another book and you didn't tell me. We need to schedule a book signing." Yes, ma'am.

P: Yes. It is so important to realize relationships. Victoria Christopher Murray said that her first book sales came from her sorority sisters, Delta Sigma Theta. Why would you try to push yourself on people who don't know you? Going to Book Expo America is great, but the attendees don't know you or have an immediate commonality.

V: And you can't sell at Book Expo America. The booth fee is cost prohibitive for most indie authors. Booth fee, travel, meals, lodging for a multi-day event, and you can't sell. You must be strategic about what you're going to do and how you're going to get there. I couldn't sell at the Christian Retailers Show either. I was an author with Send the Light Distributor, and they gave authors time slots for book signings. I gave away 150 copies of my first book, *Blended Families: An Anthology*. I spent the first three days of the conference distributing postcards highlighting my appearance and inviting booksellers to get a complimentary autographed copy. Giving away books is part of publicity.

P: It is, so don't hoard your books. You have to give away books to the right people: influencers and decision makers.

V: Some authors spend too much to publish. It's hard to give away a book that cost $10 to print. My books cost me a dollar or two. How many do you need?

P: Yes, that part. If you're going to give away a book, include a media release, postcard, or bookmark requesting an Amazon review. Because reviews help your rankings on Amazon.

V: Absolutely. Speaking of giveaways, when I receive requests to donate items for a conference, I donate something [trinkets, PDFs] with my name and contact information on it. When I donate books for giveaways or raffles, I include a letter to the person intended to receive it requesting a review, follow on social media, and post a picture tagging me in it. You have to let people know what you want them to do.

P: One author included a checklist of things readers could do once they had her book.

> Hello, friend! Thank you for purchasing X. Here's how you can help me spread the word:

- Tell your family and friends about the book.
- Review it on Amazon, Good Reads, Barnes and Noble.
- Buy a copy for a friend.
- Share a favorite quote from the book and hashtag it.
- Encourage women to form a discussion group around the book.
- Request media outlets in your area to feature me in an interview.
- Invite me to speak at your online or onsite events.

It doesn't have to be on a piece of paper. It can be on a postcard. You have to let people know how they can help you by making it plain and easy for them.

V: Like, putting the Amazon link with the request.

P: Yes. Making sure it's easy for them. Creating a short Amazon link using Bitly.com.

V: In your experience, what is the biggest marketing challenge for authors and how do you serve them to overcome it?

P: They don't know where to find the media and they don't know what to say. I help authors find a hook for the book, so they can master the media they're trying to attract.

V: Very good. Of course, you do lots more, but that gets the momentum going to move forward.

P: Before we pitch, there are things that they have to do with their brand.

V: When I'm mentoring clients who hire me to help build their virtual brand, I start with a deep dive into their online presence. I cyber-stalk them to analyze their platforms for consistency, logo, brand, and their message. When I report my findings, they often say, "I had no idea." When I do the work to create a powerful media release and land them interviews, I want them to be findable and ready.

P: Yes. You have fourteen abandoned Facebook pages.

V: I'm working with a client who had three fan pages. I said, "These two have to go." People may be sitting there wondering what you're doing.

P: Or thinking you're out of business.

V: Or see that you only have thirty fans and assume that you don't know what you're doing, not realizing you have a couple thousand fans on the other page. The psychology of marketing. Last question, Pam. What is your favorite business resource and why?

P: I love my podcast. I share lots of information and teaching people to get out there and get known. When doing a media release targeting the African American market, I use BlackPR.com. To connect with the African American Christian audience, I use <u>BlackGospelPromo.com</u>. To reach a different audience, I use <u>PRNewsWire.com</u>.

V: I've used all of them. BlackPR yielded immediate, tangible results as authors registered for my in-person events. It starts with an effective media release—free of typos and fluffy content—and directed to the right media outlets. Do you help your clients write media releases or do you write them?

P: For my VIP clients, I write it for them. My Brand Accelerator clients receive templates and then I review their work. I teach them because "you can give a person a fish, feed them for a day or teach them how to fish and feed them for a lifetime."

V: Lao Tzu! That's my favorite quote.

P: Knowing how to pitch to media, who to pitch, and what to say. Authors should be comfortable with that.

V: Absolutely. Pam, thank you so much. Authors, seasoned or novice, have more insight into what's needed to market their bestseller, stay relevant with media, and be ready with that pitch to land significant attention. It starts local and expands out.

P: Yes. Never despise small beginnings. You never know, a major newspaper editor may read about you in the local paper.

V: Or his cousin reads it, and says, "Cuz, you have to do something with this hometown hero." You don't know where it's coming from, so be open to all things.

Pam, thank you for sharing this invaluable information.

P: My pleasure.

Pam Perry is an award-winning communications professional. She mentors authors, speakers, and entrepreneurs to build platforms and attract major media and publishers. She is the publisher of *Speakers Magazine* and founder of the National Association of Black Podcasters. She has been featured in many major publications (including several covers), and on more than 100 radio and TV programs. She authored *Synergy Energy: How to Use the Power of Partnerships to Market Your Book, Grow Your Business and Brand Your Ministry,* and *115 PR Tips on How to Brand Your Ministry.* Known as the master of connecting the right people, for the right project, at the right time, Pam Perry PR works hard to help her clients' brand—and get paid—like a superstar.

<u>Connect with Pam</u>
PamPerryPR.com
Amazon.com/author/pamperry
Facebook.com/PamPerryPRPage
Linkedin.com/in/PamPerryPRCoach
Twitter.com/PamPerry

<u>Pam's Favorite Resource</u>
<u>HubSpot.com</u> has amazing software products for inbound marketing, sales, and customer service. Their trainings on digital marketing are phenomenal.

Optimizing Your Amazon Author Page

Carolyn Howard-Johnson

V: Joining me today is award-winning poet, novelist, and former publicist, Carolyn Howard-Johnson. Carolyn helps authors with nitty-gritty, "how-tos" to get nearly free publicity. She shows authors how to do what their publishers can't or won't, which is priceless for independent authors. We met at the Erma Bombeck Humor Writers' Conference. She presented at my 2007 conference for aspiring authors.

I used one of her strategies from *The Frugal Book Promoter: How to Do What Your Publisher Won't* to land a feature in the *Dayton Daily News*. For no cost—other than my time and nerves—an article with my name, business information, and website was circulated to over 300,000 people in print. The article pertained to the publishing workshops I hosted for inmates in a local institution.

Carolyn, you have a wealth of information on marketing and promotions. I want to focus on how to optimize your Amazon author page. You have over twenty books in various formats on your Amazon author page. Tell us about an Amazon author page.

C: First of all, it's free. Amazon sells more books than anybody else in the world. Your book must be available for purchase on Amazon and then you can claim your author page at Author.Amazon.com. Get your page in good shape and use it often to boost your ranking. Every time you write a book review, the hyperlink links back to your author page. My books, my Twitter stream, my bio, and one of my blogs are there. It's like having your own website on Amazon.

I use a simplified, shortened link to advertise my page. You can leave it up to Amazon to send people there, but why do that, right?

V: Note that your author page does not replace your website. Like Facebook, Amazon changes often. You need to have your own place for people to connect with you. This amazing Amazon service helps readers get to know and follow you like other social media platforms. You can manage all your books in one place and get insight into your sales performance. Amazon doesn't share proprietary information like who purchased from you, but you can track your sales by title, format, and state of purchase.

During discovery calls with authors who hire me to help them sell more books, I search for their books like a potential reader. Oftentimes, I can't find their books on Amazon because they have a common title, no subtitle, or a common name. If people can't find you in the first couple of pages, they're not going to keep searching.

Just because you have a book on Amazon doesn't mean you automatically have an author page. I didn't realize that helping an author with a review helped me, too.

C: It's a two-way street when you claim your author page. I have a book on reviews that covers everything you need to know about managing your Amazon reviews. My Amazon page is bit.ly/CarolynsAmznProfile (case sensitive).

V: My Amazon author page URL is Amazon.com/author/valeriejlewiscoleman. If Amazon hasn't changed the algorithm, authors can customize their URL on the dashboard. Creating your Amazon URL versus using the generated series of letters and numbers that Einstein couldn't remember was brilliant. You customized it using Bit.ly and included AMZN for Amazon. Great idea. TinyURL.com also creates shortened links.

C: Here's another secret. If you sign up as an affiliate (Affiliate-Program.Amazon.com), every time somebody uses your link to buy a book, Amazon gives you a percentage. Not very much, but it can add up.

V: Absolutely. I'm launching an online mastermind, Pen of the Writer Academy. One of the bonuses for participants is inclusion in the Pen of the Writer Wall of Fame; a virtual bookstore tied to Amazon.

C: If you're writing nonfiction, you can use the affiliate link in your books, too. However long you can keep your book alive, that book is earning a bit of money for you.

V: The cross-promoting review feature is phenomenal.

C: Be careful not to promote yourself in the review because Amazon is working hard to keep reviews credible. They don't want paid reviews or insider reviews from mom.

V: If Amazon finds that you have bogus reviews or operated dishonestly, they will shut you down. Integrity is critical. Authors are using deceitful tactics to boost their ranking, cheating. Any award or accolade I get; I want it to be genuine because I earned it. I know of authors who intentionally put their book in the wrong category to elevate their ranking on the bestseller's list.

C: Bad idea. Ticking off readers and trying to trick Amazon. So, readers buy your book, which is not what they expected and leave a bad review.

V: You might make a sale and hit the bestsellers list by tricking people, but the long-term affect is not good.

C: Don't try to break the system, work with it.

V: Yes. Amazon has a great system. My novel, *The Forbidden Secrets of the Goody Box*, released, a month or two from Steve Harvey's book, *Act Like a Lady, Think Like a Man*. Since both books are about dating and relationships, my book popped up as "You may also like…" when people bought his book. The more legitimate reviews you get, the more work Amazon does for you.

C: Yes. Your keywords are really important. You want to select categories that are true to your book and enticing. You can have two or three categories, so choose those that best describe your book and have the least competition. When you pair the two, you can authentically boost ratings.

Let's say you rank in the top ten in your category. You're going to promote the promotion, right? You're going to tweet the achievement.

V: Screenshot when you hit the top 100 for proof and bragging rights. It makes a difference when you position your book in a niche category instead of general nonfiction. By strategically reducing the number of books in a category, you boost your opportunity to be a bestseller. I also found that Amazon's algorithm puts my books in other categories that people used to find them.

C: They're likely to do that if you sold lots of books or you have other things contributing to the algorithm. Everything you do on Amazon nudges your book's algorithms.

V: That makes sense. When I publish anthologies (*Do It Right the First Time* is my fifth), I encourage contributors to add the book to their Amazon author page. The book appears on thirty author pages as opposed to just mine. When readers click on the book, it'll show the list of contributors. If they claimed their author page at Author.Amazon.com, the hyperlink takes readers to their page with their bio, books, and more. It's a way to keep momentum using the cross-promotion strategy.

C: Yes. You might have a couple of active authors out of the bunch. If you get five percent who actively promote, you're doing well.

There's some misinformation about anthologies including that the contributors don't get anything from it. That's absolutely false. If you utilize anthologies properly, they can be great for your credibility.

Another thing—not just with anthologies—when you help an author who mentions you in their acknowledgements, talk about it. Tweet it. Post it on Facebook. You're proud, you're excited, it's fun. I have two shelves filled with books that have mentioned me in acknowledgements or quoted me. That little shelf does more than brag. When I feel crappy, I look at that shelf and say, "Look at how many other authors my books have helped. I'm doing something important."

V: Absolutely. You have that much influence. You gave me an endorsement for my book: *Self-Publishing Made Easy: Purposeful Publishing.* (https://bit.ly/3zwRiBx case sensitive)

C: Did I give you an endorsement?

V: Did you give me an endorsement? You said, "At last! A book I can recommend to others who need a guide to true self-publishing. Carolyn Howard-Johnson, author of multi award-winning *The Frugal Book Promoter*."

I sell this book when I speak at live events. When people purchase my books or bundles, your information is there in the front. You're the first of six or seven reviews. That's another great strategy for authors: endorsements and reviews for transference of credibility. I first heard you speaking at Erma Bombeck Humor Writers Conference. You explained how you took aspects of your novel, *This is the Place*, and got publicity and notoriety in your Utah community. Even though it takes time to create that momentum, it positions you, especially in this digital age of online magazines and newspapers, you are out there in perpetuity.

C: I sent query letters with feature ideas to local press and other media and did pretty well. I got an article in one of the big newspapers in LA. I didn't hear from my local newspaper, which is associated with the *LA Times*. Just like everybody else, I'm a bit shy about making the call. It's easier to send an email. I sat at a desk at a newspaper, so I know they need content. I forced myself to call the local editor. They figured that it didn't need to run because it had already published in LA. I said, "The book is about tolerance and we're having problems right here in our hometown." They agreed and sent a photographer to take a picture of me with my old typewriter. It ran on the front page in color.

Did I stop there? No. I called three friends and asked them to write a letter to the editor. I didn't tell them what to say. Three days later, their letters were on the opinion page in black and white. So, my article got double publicity. Print media is not dead. It still holds a cachet that online doesn't have. Don't be afraid to send a media release to online, print, radio, and TV media.

V: That's great. I used to laminate every article that was printed about me, but then it got to be too many. Do you keep the printed articles? It's easy to do it digitally by grabbing the link.

C: Yes. Sometimes the links go dead. I have a big cardboard box that I stuffed with articles, but it got to be too much.

V: You can scan and add them to your electronic press kit (EPK), your speaker one sheet, your website, and social media.

C: You should have a media room on your website. Authors can download my media kit at <u>HowToDoItFrugally.com</u>. I have one for my poetry and fiction, and one for nonfiction.

V: Absolutely. I followed a few speakers who have their speaker one sheet, speaking topics, and pre-booking questionnaire on their sites. A couple of the websites have printable, customizable flyers, so all the event host has to do is print. One guy had cut-and-paste media releases and emails for his clients to use. With his permission, the communications were shared to promote his appearance. Everything an event planner needs to host you at an event can be on the website.

C: You can create a short link and put it in the bio of your Amazon author page.

V: That's a great idea. I purchase URLs from <u>GoDaddy.com</u> and then redirect them to a specific page on <u>PenOfTheWriter.com</u>. For this anthology, DoItRightTheFirstTime.com was $2,500, so I bought <u>DoItTheFirstTime.com</u> for $10 a year.

C: Great idea.

V: It saves money by not hosting multiple websites. I don't need twenty SSL certificates when one will do. I have two websites and multiple landing pages. <u>FreeYourMindWritersRetreat.com</u>, <u>PowerBookFest.com</u>, <u>ThingsICanBe.com</u>, <u>TheGoodyBoxBook.com</u> are URLs that go to specific pages on one website, <u>PenOfTheWriter.com</u>.

C: I bought all the possibilities for my name early on because I didn't want to have to buy them from somebody at $2,500 if I ever got famous.

V: As I walk clients through the publishing process, most times they don't have a website. If they do have a website, it's typically not their name. If possible, purchase the URL of your name, business name, and book from GoDaddy. It's easier when you're doing an interview to direct listeners to the page with a URL that aligns with your message.

C: That's why it's so important to get your name first. HowToDoItFrugally.com fits my brand, but it doesn't fit all the other work I'm doing. That goes for your Twitter and Facebook handles. Try to use your name. Plus, it keeps somebody else from using it.

V: Absolutely. It's important to get your domain as soon as possible. With my female clients, we discuss the name that they are going to use to brand themselves. One of my clients, April Foster, is using her middle name. For one, her book is *Lynn's Itchy Skin* and we want readers to connect the story to her. Also, April Lynn Foster is less common, which makes her more searchable on Google.

C: That brings us back to Amazon. It's a huge search engine that has been compared to Google. It's the biggest search engine for books, so you want to make sure that you get the right name for your author page. I still use the same AOL email address because I don't want to lose anybody. If I changed addresses, you may not have found me to work together again. Making people work more than they need isn't good. Make it easy for them.

V: That's a do-it-right-the-first-time strategy. Make sure your social media handles are the same or as close as possible. One reason why I couldn't find authors was the name they use was not used on the book. Be consistent. My professional name is Valerie J. Lewis Coleman for identifying and differentiating me from all the other Valerie Colemans in the world. One Valerie Coleman is a master flutist who takes the first ten pages in a Google search. I added my maiden name so friends from high school and college, who knew me before I got married, can still find me.

C: In my book, *How to Get Great Book Reviews, Frugally and Ethically,* I have an entire chapter on how to manage your reviews on Amazon including a case study on how reviews affect book sales.

V: You must be strategic about how readers post reviews. Amazon separates verified reviews — books purchased from their site — from unverified ones. All those things play into how you move up in the ranks. Lots to know about Amazon, but you have to be there. It's not an option. Other than books sales, what ways can an author leverage their Amazon author page?

C: Credibility. It's about showing up. As an author, you are branding yourself. Like when you worked with the inmates. We're telling something about who we are no matter what book we're selling. You want people to identify with you in certain ways, so branding is super important. You want your Amazon page to do the same thing for you, which is another reason you don't want to bad-mouth another book. You may hate the book, but do not slash and burn another book or author. Tell your neighbor, if you must, but don't post it for the public to see. When you put something on the web, you're letting yourself show.

V: People can be very judgmental, so you have to be mindful of what you put out there. Keep focused on your brand, your intention, and how you want the public to perceive you. Think about how you would feel if somebody gave you a one-star review. Whether deserving or to cause harm, it's hurtful and can damage your reputation and Amazon ranking. People may decide to not buy your book because of your remarks on someone else's book. Since the review links back to you, the review can land on your author page.

C: Word gets around. People love to spread bad stuff. You want to avoid that negative exposure, unless you have a controversial book and you're trying to spark conversation.

V: In your experience, what is the biggest marketing challenge for authors, especially self-published authors and how do you serve them to overcome it?

C: The biggest challenge for self-published authors is coming to the realization that they have to market their book. Just because you're creative, talented, and beautiful with a wonderful book, does not mean you're above marketing. If you want your baby to suffer a swift death, dig in your heels and refuse to do the work. You might sell a few books, but not many.

If you're in this business to help a large number of people, entertain, make a fortune, or whatever your goal, you have to market. Even if you are not self-published, book publishers don't have marketing budgets like they once did. The budget they do have goes to Stephen King, not new authors. You need to partner with the marketing professional the publisher assigns or be knowledgeable enough to hire a marketing professional. Tattoo this on your forehead: nobody knows your book like you do. If you're not active in your own promotion, your marketing campaign will suffer. Your book continues to need you.

V: In perpetuity, if you want to keep selling. My first book, *Blended Families: An Anthology*, came out in 2006. Although I'm not actively promoting it, it sells because people see it on my Amazon author page. If they like one book, they're willing to try another.

Carolyn, what service do you provide to help authors overcome this misunderstanding of marketing?

C: I consult, but I try to talk myself out of a job first. Depending on what's needed, I refer authors to one of my books. You want to connect with people who know what they're doing, so you're not learning from one of these fly-by-nights, non-credible "experts."

V: How to make a million dollars in three days.

C: Yes. Find somebody who's been around a while, knows what they're doing and learn from them. Don't read just one book. Get several perspectives.

V: I heard that if you read and comprehend seven books in a specific topic, you become a subject matter expert in that topic.

C: That seems like a good rule of thumb. Do you have any children's authors in your group?

V: I'm a children's author now. I published *Oh, The Things I Can Be When I See Me* (ThingsICanBe.com) with my granddaughters. I published children's books for clients and a chapter book is in the pipeline.

C: Okay. I have an author for you to read as one of your seven: Karen Cioffi-Ventrice. She's a children's book author and wrote *How to Write a Children's Fiction Book*. I also like *Crafting Dynamic Dialogue: The Complete Guide to Speaking, Conversing, Arguing, and Thinking in Fiction* by Writer's Digest.

V: Thank you for those resources. Last question: what is your favorite resource and why?

C: *The Frugal Book Promoter: How to Get Nearly Free Publicity on Your Own or By Partnering with Your Publisher*. It was originally self-published. The new hardback version is published by Modern History Press.

V: Whether you do it yourself or hire somebody for your marketing and promotions, you need to know what they should be doing for you.

C: They can't write a query letter for you until you tell them what to put into it.

V: Absolutely. When I first got into the business, a publicist was charging authors $5,000 a month. I don't know what she did for the authors, but she mailed me copies of authors' books. For that investment, she should have been more strategic about who received review copies. I appreciated the books, but they should have gone to media, bookstores, and libraries. That's a hefty price to miss the mark.

C: When my aunt died, she left me $35,000. I used it to hire a publicist. She didn't do anything for me that I couldn't do for myself. Another mistake made when hiring a publicist is failing to choose someone who makes individual contacts. That's wonderful if they know somebody at the *Today Show*. If they don't have a solid list with the right people interested in your genre, it could be a waste of money. Even if they've been in business twenty years, make sure they have experience with authors and publishers who work in your genre.

The Frugal Book Promoter has information on how to hire a publicist, questions to ask, and where to get the best kind of information. If I want an editor, I'm not going to hire a college grammar professor or an English Lit person. They may know grammar well, but they have never written dialogue or fiction.

V: Right. They're not a developmental editor.

C: They don't know anything about the publishing industry. Ask for references. You have to screen service providers at least as well as you screen a plumber you're hiring to work on your home.

V: You have to invest money and time. A book is only going to be as good as you make it. Garbage in, garbage out. You can't drop your manuscript into a magical machine that cranks out bestsellers. Technology has made it easy to be a published author. Push 'submit' and you're live on Kindle. But it wasn't professionally edited, the cover is crappy, and it's overpriced. Then they wonder why books aren't selling.

C: *The Frugal Editor* gives information on how to maximize front and back matter, how to save tons of time, and how to partner with your editor.

V: You don't know what you don't know.

C: Yeah. Pay a bit more and get the expertise. When clients come to me early in the process, I can usually save them thousands of dollars on publishing alone.

V: I have a service called Print My Book (Bit.ly/POWERPrint case sensitive). Hundreds of printers from across the world bid on my book projects. As a result, I saved myself and my clients thousands of dollars. For my children's book, I got bids as high as $9 a copy. Nope. I chose a high-quality printer and got the books for just over $2 a copy. If I didn't have options and spent that extra $7 gap on a thousand books, that's $7,000 wasted! Instead, it's money saved.

C: Authors often forget there must be a net profit margin in the sale of each book or they lose money and limit promotional opportunities.

V: I'm an engineer by degree. I love using left-brain problem-solving strategies to save money and make money. I teach my clients how to do it better, faster, easier, while maintaining quality. When their books are done, my clients better understand publishing. They understand what makes for a good cover. They understand how to calculate retail price. They carry Queen V Publishing's standards with them. It makes me happy to know that they have a better understanding of what is— and is not—a quality book.

C: That may be the most valuable thing I learned as a shop owner: margin. An item that costs me $2 got a $4 price tag. An employee thought we were cheating customers. I gave her a lesson on economics 101, but I don't think she understood.

It sounds crazy, but in one hour of consultation, you'll learn several things that you need to know; things you didn't know you needed to know. A session with me is $160. As a frugal person, that's a lot of money. But what I can save you is...

V: Priceless.

C: The best investment you ever made.

V: I offer 60 Minutes to Bestseller (Bit.ly/POWER60Mins case sensitive). I share tons of information, resources, checklists, samples, and anything authors need to move forward. A client used it to master writing media releases. I customized the discussion with information specific to her book and explained how she could magnify and monetize her message. She landed several online articles and paid speaking engagements as a result of distributing a media release the right way. Anybody can put out a media release just like anybody can publish a book, but doing it the right way will get you a higher level of results. Working with someone who has proven results and systems will save you thousands. You'll easily save ten times the investment by doing it right the first time. Avoiding common mistakes, access to reliable resources, and then yielding repeatable results. It's worth the money.

C: Think of all the time you put into that gorgeous, perfect book of yours. Are you going to spend a lifetime just dreaming about it? Or publish it only to come away from the experience disappointed?

V: Lots of writers get stuck saying, "I don't know how to," "I don't know where to start," or "I don't know what to do." When you hire the right person, you break through the excuses, overcome pitfalls, and finish the book. To do it right the first time, you want to connect with people who have already done what you hope to do and did it well. Carolyn, thank you so much for being part of this project.

C: My pleasure.

Carolyn Howard-Johnson brings her experience as a publicist, journalist, and editor to the advice she shares in her *How to Do It Frugally Series*. These books for writers have won awards from USA Book News, Readers' Views, Next Generation Indie Books, and the coveted Irwin Award. She is the recipient of the California Legislature's Woman of the Year in Arts and Entertainment Award, and her community's Character and Ethics Award for her work promoting tolerance. She was named on Pasadena Weekly's list of "Fourteen San Gabriel Valley women who make life happen," and was given her community's Diamond Award for achievement in the arts. For ten years, Carolyn shared her expertise as an instructor for UCLA Extension's world-renown writers' program.

<u>Connect with Carolyn</u>
HowToDoItFrugally.com
Bit.ly/CarolynsAmznProfile
Facebook.com/CarolynHowardJohnson
Twitter.com/FrugalBookPromo

<u>Carolyn's Favorite Resource</u>

The Frugal Book Promoter: How to Get Nearly Free Publicity on Your Own or By Partnering with Your Publisher because it has information on how to hire a publicist, create your media kit, and build your mailing list.

Attracting the Masses to Your Message

Sulondia "SueHam" Hammond

V: Joining me today is award-winning writer, entertainer, and community leader, Sulondia "SueHam" Hammond. She provides quality entertainment in the form of stage plays and films, and helps authors connect their message to the masses. She made two TV appearances on the *Steve Harvey Show*. SueHam and I shared the stage at several Red Ink Conferences.

We're going to talk about brand and its importance. SueHam, as if you are not already uber busy with your entertainment empire, you just landed the office of councilwoman and have the keys to the city of Kingstree, South Carolina.

Congratulations. I'm sure that your brand and what you're doing with your business helped you posture yourself to land that role. Would that be a fair assumption?

S: Oh, yes. Marketing played a key role. Marketing is like breathing; it has to be done. People say, "I don't have a business. How am I marketing?" If you're selling something, then you are a marketer. Call yourself a salesperson or marketer, but you're always selling. As someone who markets educational and financial programs and advocates for the community, marketing definitely gave me a leg up when it came to running for office.

V: What did you apply to the campaign that will be out-of-the-box for authors considering their marketing strategies?

S: Direct mailing. I found that to be beneficial, especially in a rural area. People say that email is dead, but it's not true. You're still checking it on your phone. The open rates may not be as high. Text messaging is definitely the way to go, which we did. But I found that people still go to their mailbox, whether it's a post office box or at the end of a driveway. The best way for us to reach everybody was to combine direct mailers with text messaging. And we went old school. We handed out flyers in public places. We went where the people were. We knocked on doors in the middle of COVID. Of course, we used COVID-safe practices.

We delivered cleaning supplies and food. I live in a rural area that's pretty impoverished. They were very thankful. When we came to the homes of elderly, they were excited to have somebody knocking on the door.

Social media was a saving grace for me, especially for the people we couldn't reach by telephone, email, or mailbox.

V: Good for you! I have not used direct mail, but I worked with a couple authors who used it. They purchased lists by zip code. How did you get your mailing lists?

S: Political organizations mail those lists, but you can Google where to find them. They're amazing because once I have the addresses, not only can I send political stuff, but now I can send stuff that pertains to my business. I love it.

V: We had bad addresses bounce back because we didn't buy from the post office or political campaigns. I guess that should be expected. One thing we did to cut costs was mailed postcards as opposed to something placed in envelopes. The postage is considerably cheaper.

S: Correct. And not only that, people are going to see it. They may not open the mail because we can readily identify spam.

V: That's a bill, I don't want that.

S: Right! So, we toss it without opening it. But when we get an attractive postcard with bright colors, you're going to look at it. You might toss it afterwards, but you're still going to look at it.

Something else I wanted to throw out there are robotic or robocalls; automated calls to people. Many times, people think that only happens for political campaigns or telemarketing, but what if you tell people in your community about your business? They're familiar with you and may not feel like you're spamming. They're relatively cheap at less than two cents a call.

V: What services did you use for your mass text messaging and robocalls? I knew about text-messaging services, but I never thought about doing automatic calls.

S: RoboDial.org. I called seven or eight hundred people for like $25.

V: That's affordable. You had to upload the numbers?

S: Yes. I had a list I uploaded as an Excel spreadsheet and recorded my own messages. I'm using this tool for my stage plays and community events. For text messaging, I used Txt180.com/sl/22m.

V: Great resources for authors or anyone wanting to expand their marketing reach. You could spend way more than $25 and still not hit your intended audience.

S: Absolutely. The text messaging for 500 messages was something like $19 a month.

V: That's affordable!

S: People check their text messages.

V: Define brand and then tell me about yours. When people think Sulondia Hammond or "SueHam," what specifically is your brand?

S: Brand is what people think of you, your reputation, and the first thing that comes to their mind. Every three or four months, I want to make sure that I'm conveying the right message about my brand. On Facebook, I ask people to name the top three things they think of when they see my face or hear my name. Many times, we think we're conveying a certain message, but it may not be received by the public in the way that we want. My brand should represent excellence, entertainment, education, and enlightenment. When people say, "I see you as a motivator, investor, speaker, writer, or producer of stage plays," I know that my brand is getting out there in the way that I want. Brand is your reputation and what people know you for.

V: That's good. I like that you said, "Excellence, education, entertainment, and enlightenment." An alliteration of e's makes it easy to remember.

Simple is better. The word "POWER" can be pulled from my company, **P**en **O**f the **W**rit**ER**. I empower and educate authors. Last year, I came up with an acronym for **RISE** because I get clients **R**esults through my **I**ntegrity, **S**ervice, and **E**xcellence.

S: I love that!

V: Excellence and integrity are important to me. Lots of people get into this business just to take advantage of people. They take your money or produce junk on your behalf. I do not have time for junk.

S: I dislike people who are not genuine, not passionate about what they do, and just chasing the dollar. Typically, when you're chasing money, your services are mediocre and lackluster.

V: Absolutely. I tell my clients that they should know what they're writing about. You're picking a hot topic like bullying, human trafficking, or opioids. No! If it's not your passion, don't do it because it'll come out in your message. And you won't be as effective because you're not writing about your passions, feelings, and experiences. Don't chase the dollar. If you do it right, the dollars will find you.

S: It might take a little time, but it will be worth it. But you'll have the longevity. You burn out quickly because you got it fast, and it wasn't authentic. When you're serious and authentic, you're going to have longevity. You know what to do and passion will have you wanting to do it until you die.

V: Absolutely. It's an if-you-could-do-anything-you-wanted-and-not-worry-about-money or what-would-you-be-willing-to-do-even-if-you-didn't-paid-for-it passion. Those things represent your passion and what you should write about. Write about what you know. I know people get paid to write research papers, but it's very mechanical. It's not personalized, transparent, vulnerable, or genuine. As a result, it may not be as transformative for your intended readers.

SueHam is dropping these nuggets! I agree with you when it comes to excellence. Your brand represents your reputation. People mention brand, but then they don't really speak to what it means. I was at a coffee shop when a lady pointed and said, "Hey, you're Pen of the Writer!" She didn't know my name, but she knew my company and that was okay with me. Part of the brand is your logo, colors, and how you want to be perceived in the world.

We talked about street marketing; the grassroots efforts for the campaign, but what other strategies do you use to reach the media to boost your brand?

S: Before I had the money to hire a PR person to draft a media release for me, I did it the old-fashioned way. I visited sites and submitted my story. I told them who I was, I had written a book, and that I would love to talk about it on their platform. Surprisingly, they responded by requesting my availability on specific dates. I had to be clear and concise about why my message was a good fit for their station. The last thing a producer wants is to have you choke on air or you give yes, no, and I-don't-know answers. Through that email, I conveyed that I spoke well by including links to videos. I wanted to reassure that I wouldn't embarrass them or me.

I Googled news stations. I contacted newspapers, magazines, and blogs. When social media posts requested guest experts, I submitted myself on behalf of myself.

V: They need content. That's how they get paid.

S: Absolutely. Then I went to major TV stations with snippets of interviews from local TV stations. Why not national TV and radio? At first, I wasn't getting any hits, so I started my own show. I interviewed people to get access to their audiences while they got access to mine. I in boxed prominent people and asked to interview them. I built my credibility and was able to interview ET the Hip-Hop Preacher, Lisa Nichols, Dr. Dennis Kimbro, and others. I continued to create content including videos of me being silly.

V: Where did you post these videos?

S: YouTube, Twitter, Facebook. I did very little on LinkedIn because it is a more serious platform for professionals. Facebook and YouTube were my bread and butter and then I added Instagram. Videos were comical, business, or inspirational, but the one that got millions of views and led to the Steve Harvey interview was a beat-boxing video. I made silly noises with my mouth and acted crazy.

V: I saw that video before I met you. Hilarious. Your blonde hair looked gray, so I thought you were a beat-boxing granny.

S: I told Maurice to keep filming until I said, "Cut!" I'm dressed for church beat boxing and staged the fall at the end. My clothes got dirty. A year after I uploaded the videos, it got some traction and appeared on World Store Hip Hop. From there, the video went viral. When *The Steve Harvey Show* was fairly new, I went to the site for the TV show, clicked on be a guest, and made my pitch. I included the video with millions of views and within thirty minutes a producer contacted me.

V: Wow. Your timing was perfect. Had you contacted them with no real traction on your video, it may not have had as much credibility, power, or influence on her.

S: That is so true. With COVID restrictions, everybody's doing interviews via Zoom. It's so easy to be a guest on shows now because you don't have to travel. It's a great time to say that you have a book relevant to what's going on today or just pitch to producers. Have your media release in order, the who, what, where, when, why and how, and upload it to HARO. I learned about the site a year ago.

V: Help a reporter out or <u>HelpAReporter.com</u>.

S: You can subscribe to get requests that match your expertise for radio, TV, newspapers, magazines, and blogs. The internet is amazing. There's no reason why anyone should not be interviewed whether national, local, blog, or podcast, which is really popular.

V: Other than they're afraid to speak, which I find that to be the case for many authors. They just want to say, "Go buy my book. It's on Amazon." That doesn't work.

S: It does not work. Organizations like the titles of my books and invite me to speak. After I speak, I don't have to ask them to buy my books. They just do.

V: That's an important nugget. Speaking engagements, when done right, connect you with the audience. They feel your energy. When they know you, understand your background, and why you do what you do, they're more inclined to buy your book. You don't have to say, "I have books in the back of the room." They're ready to line up to take a piece of you home.

You talked about connecting with local media. When *Living Dayton* launched on NBC, I pitched my citywide book event to them. I went online, completed the form, and got a call to be on the show. It's fairly easy, but you must have a great pitch. Talk a little about the content and format of a pitch.

S: This goes back to writing about something you're passionate about because then it's easier to pitch. You can hear how excited I am about telling people how to get publicity. Many businesses suffer and even fail because no one knows they exist. It's not cool being the best kept secret.

With the best pitch, you have to tell them what problem you solve and present yourself like you've done this before, even if it's your first time. Make sure your social media reflects what your book is talking about or whatever message you want to deliver. Producers interview you before they interview you by studying your social media profiles. If you have a website, that's better. I know people who believe that they don't need a website with social media. Not true. Social media is a great introduction: how are you doing? Nice to meet you, but let's go where we really get to know each other. Let's have a few more dates on my website. You can tune into my blog, watch videos, and learn more about me.

Present yourself like you know what you're talking about and you're passionate about it. Be concise. Another thing I like to do is give a media kit that includes my bio, a picture of my book because you're going to display it on TV, and questions for the interviewer to ask me. I still do that with some people because they are interviewing three or four people a day. They are tired, busy, and have so much going on. If you present them with the questions that you want to be asked, you solve two problems. They don't have to come up with something because they haven't read your book, and you ensure that you convey to the public what you want to convey.

V: And you know the answers. It just makes sense. You want to make it as easy as possible to get connected to media and get that exposure. Develop that relationship and make them feel like you're a reliable subject matter expert.

S: Correct. When you're emailing them, don't just say, "I wrote a book, I want to be on your show." Imagine a different approach.

> I'm so-and-so. I published [insert book
> title] about [insert specific topic]. I'm an
> expert in this field with the following
> results [insert results from clients,

reader testimonials, etc.]. I'd like to be a guest on your show to discuss [insert pain point] because this problem is happening in America. This book speaks to that issue and how we can work together to solve it. I have included the book blurb and questions you can ask me should I be invited to your show.

Include your bio, website, and social media handles. You will probably get a call or email much faster than a person who says, "I just wrote a book. I want to be on your show. What do I need to do?" I get that type of requests all the time and shoot straight past them. If you don't care enough to give me more information, then why should I invest my time to pull that out of you. I don't have time for that.

Give it all to them in one scoop. I learned that from a producer at one of the shows. Have all your stuff together because they don't have time to go back and forth. If they need something else, they'll let you know.

V: Like you said, it's important to have your social media together. You don't want to look like a rump shaker on Facebook and then want to speak about wholesomeness with Jesus. Your profile page is misaligned with your brand.

My husband was stationed in Tacoma, Washington for two years. He connected with the lady who ran the children's library on the military base. He didn't have my promotional stuff with him, so I emailed him a sample of *Oh, The Things I Can Be When I See Me* and a companion activity book. He emailed it to her along with my website and she called him back in five minutes asking when I could get there for a signing. It's all tied together. People think they can act crazy on Facebook and look professional on LinkedIn. Absolutely not, especially if they Google you.

S: That's another great thing about getting interviews. I love radio, but unless a radio station is cataloging shows on the internet, once you do the interview it's over. Most TV shows, blogs, and magazines, post online so it's there forever. Don't get caught up with only doing a certain type of media. Do everything available. You can't get enough media.

V: Do them all! You define your topics of expertise and HARO sends you an email with all the journalists and reporters looking for experts. I landed newspaper articles, magazine write-ups, and interviews on TV and radio. It's a great resource.

S: Once you have the interview, you can put it on your website and share it on social media to build your credibility. You can also send it to other media outlets to show that you have done media. Because producers and show hosts are more prone to put you on when you've done it already.

V: Repurpose content. Absolutely. It's a no-brainer. If you've already been on ABC, NBC, CBS, Fox, we want you on here, too. I did an Atlanta book launch for *Oh, The Things I Can Be When I See Me* because one of my grandbabies who's in the book lives there. I had so many things going on, that I didn't contact media. My friend and accountability partner suggested that I email local media. I didn't have time to write a full media release, but she said, "Just send an email." You can't coach yourself. Sometimes, you need somebody to tell you what you need to do.

I found five or six media outlets and compiled a brief email about three sentences. The subject line was Four-Year-Old Girl Launches Debut Book. I sent the email and didn't get a response. The event was at a public library. I stepped out of the meeting room for a few minutes. When I returned, a guy with a gigantic camera and lights was in the room. At first, I was confused, until I remembered the email I sent a few hours earlier. He was with 11 Alive News and got footage. They featured us that evening. I grabbed the YouTube link (YouTube.com/watch?v=tijbGvh2_qE). I added it to my email signature, website, and presentations to aspiring authors. The forty-second video includes my website, the book cover, and my grandbaby. Once it's there, it's there.

S: I caught that nugget about the subject line. It's very important to have something catchy to make them want to open your email. A four-year-old author is amazing! Nobody has any excuses! That's a good nugget.

V: It's also important to note that just because you put something out there one, two, or fifteen times and you don't get a response, that doesn't mean you stop trying. Sometimes stations have so much going on with world events that local stuff isn't priority. Your book may get pushed to the back burner, but that doesn't mean you stop your momentum. Stay in touch with producers and develop relationships with them. Now let's get into your experiences with Steve Harvey. Authors want to know how you landed the *Steve Harvey Show*, not once, but twice.

S: Absolutely. I went to the show's website and filled out the form to be a guest for the segment something strange, or strange things people do. It was questions about address, age, upload your picture, why I wanted to be on the show. The form requested a link, so I put the link to my viral beatbox video. The video was my pitch because I couldn't come up with one. Thirty minutes later, I get a call from a 312 number. It was a producer of the show. She said, "Hi. I'm calling from the *Steve Harvey Show*. Did you submit a guest request?" I was like yeah right.

She said, "No, I'm serious. It was the beatboxing video. We really liked it and think it would be great for the segment. It has to go to three levels of producers. If everyone likes it, we'll fly you here in a couple of days, pay for the flight, lodging, and ground transportation."

V: In a couple of days? That's fast turn-around.

S: Very fast. You have to be available and may need to reschedule or drop other things on your calendar. I got a call in a day and a half. "Sue, the second producer liked it, but the third producer, not so much." My heart dropped. She said, "We'll keep your information. If we come up with something that you are a fit for, we'll call you." In my mind, I'm like yeah right.

I had her email and number, so I kept sending videos of me doing different things. Then I thought she might block me and send my emails to spam so, I went back to what got me the first call. I submitted videos sporadically for about two years.

V: Two years? You kept pumping content into that pipeline.

S: I kept pumping into the pipeline and social media. Because I believed that something's going to work. Two years later, I got a call from a different producer. He said, "Sue, about two months ago — this is their concept of a time because it had been two years — you did a beatboxing video as a church lady going to church. We've been looking at the stuff you sent us. We went to your website and didn't realize you did all this other stuff. We want to bring you on the show." At that point, I didn't want to have my first national appearance for beat boxing. That was two years ago, and I was in a different space.

V: It didn't align with your brand.

S: Right. It was not worth it. He said, "We still have to vet you. Our main producer will call you." I'm still iffy, but I was not turning it down…yet. The main producer called me. He kept me on the phone close to twenty minutes asking questions. He said, "I know you did the beatboxing, but if we brought you, it wouldn't be for that. It would be for the inspirational coaching videos. We have to interview a couple other people, but we'll get back with you." Hallelujah! Next thing I know, I got an email welcoming me to Chicago. It included travel and lodging details, and when to expect car service to the studio. I asked if I could bring family members. They said, "Sure; however, you have to cover their travel expenses."

I brought my sister and boyfriend. It was amazing to see my name on a green room. We had snacks and a TV to watch the show. I was a panelist giving a young lady relationship advice. The video promoting the upcoming segment featured me and I got lots of face time when the show premiered.

When we were leaving the NBC Studio, I got an overwhelming feeling like I'd be back, and said it to my sister and boyfriend. Let me go back. One of the things about getting on the *Steve Harvey Show* is that it was on my vision board as something I wanted to do. I had been visualizing it, and did the work to get there.

V: Work and vision go hand-in-hand.

S: Faith without works is dead.

V: You better quote that Scripture.

S: People don't understand that you exercise your faith when you work toward the goal. The entire time I was there, I was cooperative, upbeat, and kind.

V: The basics. Not uppity like I need water at exactly 72°F or I can't drink it. You're not coming back.

S: Not feeling entitled, just thankful and grateful for the opportunity. Two months later I got a call. "Sue, we're putting together another panel. We need parents to give advice to parents with teenagers. Do you have teenage kids?" I qualified! He told me that he got my info from the producer who brought me on the last time. It goes back to relationships.

V: They talk about you in the board room in a good way.

S: This time, my green room was right at the studio. I heard Steve while watching him host the show. I walked out of my green room and right into the studio. I felt closer to getting everything that I desired. I want you to understand that if you can see it, you can have it, but you have to work to achieve it.

V: Powerful. You had so many nuggets in there and the relationship part was essential. The fact that you didn't go in arrogant or entitled, but appreciative and grateful. You did the pre-work and when they checked you out to vet you, you came out on top. I'm sure many potential guests didn't make it through the vetting process. Your brand is serious, and you don't know who's watching you. Somebody can be videotaping and recording you acting a complete fool at the gas station with a scarf wrapped on your head, slippers, and PJs cussing out somebody. Next thing you know, you're viral for the wrong reasons.

Your brand is your reputation. What does your reputation say about you? When people hear your name or your business — Pen of the Writer, S — they must know that you represent excellence, quality, and integrity. People know that when they work with us, they're going to get results…RISE!

S: Very important. I failed to mention that one of my episodes with Steve Harvey ran multiple times. People hit me up on Facebook asking if I had been on the show again.

V: Re-runs, replays, and reposts. TV, radio, and podcasts reuse content. Shar Halliburton (SharHalliburton.com) assisted with social media marketing for this book. When my commitment didn't allow me to review the new content she created, I asked her to repost something from a few weeks prior. We're still putting out content and still engaging the people. It may be repeat for some people, but new for others.

My claim to fame is *The Mother Love Show*. She's the former host of the TV show *Forgive or Forget*. She helped dysfunctional family members work together and resolve issues to rebuild relationships. Powerful show. Years later, she came to Dayton promoting her book. *Half the Mother, Twice the Love* was about how she managed diabetes to change her lifestyle, change her eating, and drop lots of weight.

S: Oh wow!

V: Isn't that a great title? I took the only book I had at the time, *Blended Families: An Anthology*, to meet her. I didn't know if she had a blended family, but I was going to purchase her book and gift her mine. Three years later—you have to keep putting stuff in the pipeline—I got a call. "This is Mother Love from *The Mother Love Show*." I did the same thing, "Quit playing. I don't have time." She said, "No, baby. This is Mother Love from *The Mother Love Show*." After I realized she was legit, she said, "I'm so glad your phone number is the same."

S: Because it had been so long.

V: Over three years. She needed guests to provide content for her show. Many of the people she tried to contact had dead emails, dormant websites, and disconnected numbers. She said, "I want you to come on my show and talk about your book." By this time, I had three or four more books, so I asked which book. She said, "You have more books, baby? Mail them to me."

A few weeks later, we spoke for an entire hour. The conversation started with *Blended Families: An Anthology*, but the bulk of the conversation was about *The Forbidden Secrets of The Goody Box*. She loved it and gave me a great endorsement: "A brilliant writer. I love her work. Can I have the rights to the movie?"

I asked for permission to use her endorsement. It's on the back of *The Goody Box Book*, posted at <u>TheGoodyBoxBook.com</u>, and on other promotional material. Her show was a podcast, so I downloaded it, separated into two interviews, and posted it on YouTube. I reshare the link on my website and social media. I was interviewed at no cost to me, and repurposed the content because I came out of my introverted self and talked to Mother Love.

S: Introverted?

V: Nobody believes me. SueHam, you are an extrovert all day, every day. When I'm on the stage doing my thing, it looks like I'm an extrovert; however, I'm an ambivert; an introvert who has extrovert qualities when needed. I do my dance and then go back into my shell to be alone and recharge my energy. If you're an introvert like most writers, and you want to sell books—live, virtual, or to the media—you have to get out of your shell.

S: Going back to relationships. Once you have done well on the show and built relationship, it's easy to get a return invite. For local shows, you can go back as many times as you want. I'm so thankful for the love from local television, radio, and newspapers. Anytime I have something going on, all I have to do is send a media release and they invite me back. Authors, get your foot in the door. Make a great impression and you can come back anytime you want.

V: Absolutely. I used to work with music artists who wanted to be national. I said, "National is just pockets of local. Let's start at home and connect with the local media." *Dayton Weekly News* (DaytonWeeklyOnline.com) is a Black-owned newspaper that's been around since 1993. I have relationships with the owner and contributing writers. If I send a media release, nine times out of ten, it gets printed. I have gotten my clients full-color, above-the-crease, front-page articles because of relationship and the quality of the media release. Build those relationships, stay connected to those people, and don't send them general information. Don't bombard them with miscellaneous stuff. If it's not a newsworthy media release, you might get blocked.

S: Correct. And don't despise small beginnings. When the community sees you, they're impressed.

You don't know who they're connected to and who they may be sharing it with on social media.

V: You don't know who they know. That's another pivotal thing to think about: they may not be the influencer, event organizer, or the president of the company, but their cousin, friend, or co-worker is. When they need a speaker and they've seen you on TV, they can recommend you. One of our high schools teaches various professions with a hands-on approach. They have a multi-media department. A music business associate connected me with her friend who was a teacher/show host. I did a segment on stepfamilies, and they paid me. The interview aired for years on their station and when it did, I got phone calls and emails. How did you leverage the exposure on the *Steve Harvey Show* to further build your business?

S: My credibility shot up a thousand percent. I downloaded those YouTube clips because I didn't know how long they were going to stay. I redistributed them on my websites and social media. I went to local media and said, "Hey, I was on *Steve Harvey Show* and here's proof." They wanted to book me again to discuss my experience on the show. I sold courses on how to use media to grow your business and brand.

V: You monetized that bad boy!

S: Absolutely! I got more speaking engagements. I hired mentees who were seeking the information but didn't want to buy a course. They wanted to sit at my feet and learn. The experience made me a local household name. When I created products like stage plays, people came because they saw me on the *Steve Harvey Show*.

The craziest thing: every time somebody introduces me, they say, "She was on the *Steve Harvey Show*, not once, but twice." Although it was several years ago, once you've done something phenomenal, you can claim it forever.

V: Transference of credibility goes a long way and as long as Steve Harvey is doing the Steve Harvey thing, you benefit from his name. And until the world gets to know SueHam, you're okay with using the transference of credibility. You don't know me, but you know him. Here's what I did for/with him. So, let's transfer that credibility to what I can do for you. Powerful.

I worked with Vanessa Miller Pierce, who writes Christian fiction, to produce her second novel, *Abundant Rain*, into a stage play. Between actors, original music production, lighting, stage, and sound crews, the process was way more involved than publishing a book. What tips do you have for authors who are considering producing stage plays from their books?

S: Be passionate about it. If you feel like you can't do it, then hire someone to do it for you. Hire someone who understands your story and can help convey it in the way that you want. If the story is not authentic to the way that you want it to be perceived, don't settle. Every great story starts with a great script. Just like a novel, you have to have the words, and a play is no different. Many times, people start with locking down actors and the director. Make sure the script is legit, then focus on actors, directors, and crews. When you have a great script, you can get the right actors because they'll want to be part of the project.

V: It's important to note that the script will not be exactly the same as the book. My novel, *The Forbidden Secrets of the Goody Box: Relationship Advice that Your Father Didn't Tell You and Your Mother Didn't Know,* is a little more than 55,000 words. The companion audiobook is six hours long. No one is going to sit through a six-hour stage production. You have to refine it.

S: I get that you feel everything is important, but it cannot all be on the stage. A play should not exceed two hours because then people start to get restless.

V: More than likely, you'll need to hire somebody to revise the manuscript, so you convey your message on stage. You also have to consider intermission, scene changes, and licensing permissions for non-original music, which can be a very involved process. It's not as easy as it looks to go from book to stage.

S: And another thing about book-to-stage is that you're telling the story with dialogue. If your book is more narrative than dialogue, you have to show or say what someone's thinking on the stage.

V: Yeah, it's work. I had lots of responsibilities, but my biggest responsibility was managing the stage crew. I made sure we changed scenes within 45 seconds. I had prop totes designated for each scene. I hung a three-foot-by-four-foot poster on the backstage wall that listed the scenes, characters, and props so everybody knew what needed to happen. My team wore all black so with the houselights down, we were incognito. I clapped my hands when it was time to clear the stage. One of the actors, Bryant Bentley, who's a professional SAG actor, said, "I have acted in a bunch of stage productions, but I have never seen anybody run behind the scenes like you. Girl, you're killing it!"

S: All that's in alignment with running a great show. Dressed in black because no one needs to see you moving furniture.

V: Or talking. I had a great crew. In your experience, what is the biggest marketing challenge for authors and how do you serve them to overcome it?

S: I think the biggest marketing challenge is being seen and heard. One thing I tell people is to use video and voice. Be seen and heard so people become accustomed to seeing and affiliating with your brand. People are afraid to be judged and criticized. You have to grow some thick skin and get over it. At the end of the day, some people exist simply to criticize and judge.

But understand that that's all they do. They're not producers or creators, they're just consumers. You are a producer, you're creating. No one should be able to market your brand or tell other people about your brand better than you because you created it. At the beginning, you may need help fleshing out your brand, but as you advance, you must be able to state who you are, what you do, and whom you serve. The fear of criticism and judgment is the biggest hurdle. The only way to get past the fear is to just do it. Pick up the microphone and talk. Pick up the camera and press record. Send it to your social media outlets and keep doing it.

V: You have the SueHam School of Success. Is that a tool authors can use to master marketing strategies? What do you have in there?

S: General marketing, how to get on TV and radio, how to pitch media, and how to write media releases. We have a resource of media outlets for you to contact.

V: How is your content delivered? Is it dripped? Do they have access to you or get videos?

S: It's six months access for $97. No direct access to me, but there are videos and podcasts of me and other instructors. I run specials that include a thirty-minute consultation with me and access to the school. It's really cheap.

V: Yes, it is. I'm working on Pen of the Writer Academy (<u>PenOfTheWriterAcademy.com</u>), an online resource to take aspiring authors from start to finish on how to write, publish, and market their books. It will be full of videos, templates, checklists, and live sessions with me and guest presenters. When you think of the value they get and the fact that they can use the information over-and-over, it's priceless.

S: It's time to increase it. They can also teach it like the saying, "Learn some, do some, teach some." You can learn the strategies, apply them to your project, and then package your newfound knowledge to teach others.

V: One of my favorite quotes is by Lao Tzu. "Give a man a fish, feed him for a day. Teach a man to fish, feed him for a lifetime." Once you publish a book, people want to know how you did it. That's how I got into mentoring, hosting live events, and publishing.

I'm committed to teaching people how to do things the right way so they can repeat the process and monetize it. Teaching people marketing that most folks fear or ignore creates longevity and profitability. My last question: Sue, what is your favorite resource and why?

S: Facebook. It opened doors for me. I have reached celebrities to request interviews. I reached reporters and hosts who needed experts. I put out videos; some went viral while others had 500 views. I'm inspiring the masses. I'm telling people about my products, services, and messages while monetizing my brand. Whether organically or paid ads, I encourage you to have a marketing budget. If you have an InstaGram (IG) account, you can pay for ads on Facebook and Facebook will drop the ads to your IG account. YouTube is a close second because I get paid when people watch my videos, and they stay there forever.

V: Understand how to use social media so that you can monetize it. I hired a virtual assistant who posts for me on two Facebook fan pages and IG. My problem is I go down the Facebook rabbit hole.

S: You're not the only one. I work hard so I am entitled to an occasional visit down the rabbit hole.

V: Give yourself permission for a specified amount of time. Just come back up, Alice. SueHam, thank you so much for being a part of *Do It Right the First Time*. When I launch my academy, I'm going to have you as a guest presenter for even more insight.

S: I would love that.

Writer, producer, speaker, and real estate investor are just a few things on Sulondia "SueHam" Hammond's resume. She's known for providing quality entertainment in the form of stage plays and films, as well as classes and seminars to educate the masses in theatre, real estate investing, and financial literacy. She's presented alongside Les Brown and was an expert guest on *The Steve Harvey Show*…twice.

Connect with SueHam
SueHam.com
Amazon.com/Sulondia-Hammond/e/B007T6VFWU
Facebook.com/suehambiz
Linkedin.com/in/suehammond
Instagram.com/suehambaby
Twitter.com/suehambaby

SueHam's Favorite Resource
Facebook because it opened doors to interview celebrities and be interviewed as the guest expert.

Podcasting to Leverage Your Expertise

Audrey Bell-Kearney

V: Joining me today is author of five books, chief noisemaker, and host of Good Morning Gwinnett (GMG), Audrey Bell-Kearney. She is responsible for helping entrepreneurs, especially women business owners, realize their dreams by producing and distributing digital content.

Audrey, the information that you're going to share about leveraging your expertise with a podcast is essential to new, novice, and seasoned authors. Digital is the way of the future. Your company is Noise Media Marketing. As a chief noisemaker, you've been involved with TV, radio, print, and digital media. For authors looking to get attention, what three strategies best help them maximize the media?

A: The first thing is PR. People think that with digital media, they can push PR, publicity, and media releases to the back. Those are very powerful tools that many entrepreneurs overlook because of social media. When I first started, we were scrapping and bootstrapping trying to get our business together. I read *The Personal Touch* by Terrie Williams, publicist for Eddie Murphy and Janet Jackson. Terrie said that artists must try to stand out. I went to the Dollar Store and bought a bunch of boxes, lollipops, and Valentine's Day wrapping paper. I went to Barnes and Noble and picked all the magazines that I wanted to be featured in. I wrote a media release, put it and the candy in the box and wrapped it in the paper. I sent the "gift" to the magazine publishers and landed a feature in *Heart and Soul Magazine, Essence,* and *Today's Black Woman*. I'm still waiting for *Black Enterprise*. Some platforms allow you to distribute a media release to many media outlets.

The second strategy is to be a guest on somebody's podcast. Being a guest gets you in front of an audience that you may have never met otherwise. Before you pitch to a show, look at it, listen to it to make sure it's a good fit for you. Some hosts pre-interview guests to make sure that you're a fit for their show and audience. When you pitch yourself, make sure you have a media release. Make sure your website is working.

When I started years ago, release waivers weren't a thing. Podcasting is growing rapidly, and I need to make sure that I protect myself. I put together a media packet for my producers and included a release waiver. A guy, hit me up on LinkedIn. He sent a long, but impressive, bio. I thought he'd be a great guest, so my team sent him the media packet. He said that he felt like he had a bait and switch because he couldn't sign an image release and had to be selective about what shows he did.

V: Wait. He reached out to you to be a guest, and then didn't want to sign? It's a simple release that gives you permission to use his image to promote the podcast, so he doesn't try to sue you later.

A: He feared that we were taking his intellectual property. What intellectual property? It's an interview. If you don't want your likeness to be on somebody's show, then don't pitch. My show is in a hundred countries on all the major podcasting platforms and internet TV.

That brings me to my next piece, internet TV. Many people don't know they can get on internet TV. I started my first internet television company in 2013. It was just me, one Black woman in the over-the-top (OTT) online streaming space. Today, a couple of hundred OTT channels are independently owned and they're looking for content. They need guest experts to interview on their shows.

When I first launched my channel, I sent a blast to all my entrepreneurial friends inviting them for interviews on my TV network. Great opportunity, right? I got nothing but silence. These entrepreneurs would not get on television.

I said, "God, You gave me this crazy idea. Who am I going to put on this internet TV?" He said, "Talk to women who want to be on TV." I put out an ad to aspiring actresses. Three hundred women bombarded us with headshots and bios! Independent networks are looking for great guests and good content to spotlight. People are not paying for cable anymore. They have Fire Stick, Roku, and Comcast's Xfinity.

V: One thing you said that baffled me was entrepreneurs didn't want to be interviewed. Did they believe they had "arrived," and didn't need publicity, were they introverts like most authors who didn't want to be in front of the camera, or were they in the witness protection program?

A: I started a community called The Butterfly Squad. Membership included being on TV, my podcast, and a magazine article for $57 a month. I gave members what I wished someone had given me when I started. I wanted women to participate in a weekly mastermind and help build each other. The members weren't engaging as I had hoped. Before I shut it down, I asked a member why they didn't want to take advantage of the exposure. She said "Audrey, people see all the amazing things you offer and they're not at that level. They're not ready."

V: Intimidated.

A: I had never thought about that. I also heard often, "I don't want to be on camera because I don't like the way I look or sound." I heard that so much that I self-published *Can They See You Now?* I talked about how you can be on video, even if you hate being on camera, by using screen-share and screen captures. That put people a little more at ease.

V: Public speaking is the number one fear. Fear of judgment if I say/do the wrong thing. It befuddles me that somebody would not want that level of publicity. It can be intimidating because there's so much to do. Did you create an entry-level offer to help them?

A: My attorney friend said that I was nuts for offering all that content for pennies. She has a similar package for $15,000 a year. I'm trying to reach the woman who's trying to come up. I left the package at $57, removed all the media stuff, and kept the mastermind piece. I scaled back, but the content is available to them if they need it. I know for a fact that when you have a mastermind group, mentor, or someone you can talk to, you progress faster.

V: It's good that you listened to your tribe. I post writing prompts, inspirational quotes, and strategies in my Facebook group: Free Your Mind Writers Club (Facebook.com/groups/FreeYourMindWritersClub). Most times, I don't get feedback. One day, I posted "I have a dilemma and need your help. I'm thinking about closing this group because it doesn't seem to be adding value." Members chimed in immediately. I understood that they wanted the content, but they preferred staying in the background.

Sometimes people get quiet because they don't know what to say, or they don't want to hurt your feelings. An important tool to understand whether you're writing, podcasting, or creating digital content, you have to listen to your audience.

A: It's so funny. As we're doing this interview, I want to flip and interview you. You are great. I'll be the guest today, but you have to come on my show.

V: Definitely. I saw you celebrated the 500th episode. That is fantastic! You do one show a week?

A: I do live podcasts four days a week. I just added recorded videos. When I moved to Gwinnett, outside Atlanta, I wanted to connect with the community. Since I had been podcasting since 2009, I launched the GMG podcast. I started interviewing people once a week. I added music, horoscopes, and videos to take my brand to the next level. GMG is considered a hyperlocal hybrid. I talk about Gwinnett County, but I also interview people, talk about business, and play music.

V: Do you license the music?

A: I do. I have a membership to a music licensing company. I pay $15 a month to choose songs for my playlist. I live stream the show on Facebook and Roku TV.

Here's a funny thing, putting on makeup is not my thing. Podcasting was great for me, until I realized that I was letting the TV network go to waste. I want to take the brand to a million-dollar business. What do I need to do? Video. Guests join the live show. No editing. What you get is what you get.

V: Those are the best interviews. To be clear, podcasting is only audio?

A: No, it's both. When it first started, podcasting was audio only. Then we started vlogging and now videocasting. Although you can do well with just audio, video adds a level that you can't get with audio. It's called podcasting because Apple came out with the iPod.

V: You mentioned that podcasts go both ways. As a podcast guest, authors can be subject matter experts on the topics of their books: fiction or nonfiction. They have to research shows that align with their message and then pitch the hosts on the hopes of being a guest. For the person who wants to launch a podcast and be the host, what is your advice?

A: I'm a tech geek. People shy away from podcasting because they think it's time consuming. Podcasting only takes lots of time if you edit episodes. However, you can hire a team to do that. I don't edit. My show is live, you get what you get. I'm working with a client who does not have the time to host and manage a show. I'm going to use artificial intelligence (AI) to program her message using her voice. She'll speak once and I'll create content for her. If you're an author who wants to start a podcast, but don't have the time, AI is the new thing. You talk for ten minutes, and the software synthesizes your voice to create podcasts.

You upload it to the platform and schedule it for daily, weekly, or monthly airing.

V: So instead of speaking and recording each individual episode, you put your words in the AI and it converts your words into your voice?

A: Yes. Why is that important? As an author, you can give people snippets of a chapter. You can ask probing questions that connect episodes. If they didn't hear the first few chapters, they'll buy the book. You can be elusive with this technology and build a swell so readers want more. In one sitting, you can create a thirteen-part series and schedule it to air. You can do a five-minute episode as a teaser and then turn it into an audiogram (GetAudiogram.com).

V: That oscillating bar.

A: Yes. Leverage this technology while it's pretty much free. You can start a podcast with little money on platforms like Anchor.fm. You can tell the industry is growing because Spotify, Apple, and Amazon dumped tons of money into it. Brands are launching their own podcasts. When I launched GMG two years ago, I was the only one in the area. Now the daily newspaper has a podcast, the local magazine has a podcast, and the commissioner has a podcast. It's growing and people are paying attention. As an author, podcasting is another way to share your message.

V: I'm working on client projects, hosting events, and trying to write my next book. It's tough to etch out time to create content. Combining podcasting with AI makes it much easier.

You mentioned that the pool of opportunity is expanding and is going to cost soon. How can authors use podcasting to build brand awareness, leverage their expertise, and create massive exposure?

A: If you are expert in small business development, put up a brief training on five tips to launch your small business. Break the process into small chunks for your audience to digest. It does not have to be a thirty-minute segment because people don't listen that long. You want people to get a taste of who you are, so share your expertise. People have asked, "If I'm giving it away for free, why would people pay me?" They are going to pay you because they want more of you. Even with my show running four days a week, people ask for my help. They want the expert—YOU—to help solve their problem.

The other thing is those episodes air live on Apple Podcasts, Spotify, iHeart Radio, and Amazon Music. It gives you leverage to get massive exposure across all those platforms. It is going to require you to work to build your audience. If people are not searching for you, they won't organically find you. You have to make them search for you. At the end of every show, I encourage listeners to follow me on Facebook and Instagram. Follow me on Apple and give the show five stars. Ask Alexa to open Good Morning Gwinnett. If you have an Apple iPhone, download Good Morning Gwinnett in the App Store. You have to be proactive in telling them how to find you.

V: Ask. My clients have told me that they had no idea it took all of this work to publish a book. It doesn't take much effort to half do it, sell a few books, and then not have longevity. If you want this business to be viable—not a hobby—and you want to transform lives, including your own, you have to be consistent, persistent, and relevant. I serve my clients to develop their next. After they read your book, what do you want them to do? Hire you to speak? Buy in bulk? Host a book club discussion? The Bible says that we have not because we ask not. Some people wait to be told what to do.

You said that the segments don't have to be long, drawn-out podcasts. Another reason people want to connect going forward is because in a shorter segment, you can only share who, what, where, when, and why. For how, they have to see you because it's an involved process. I cannot effectively convey years of experience in a Messenger inbox or one-hour interview. Same with you. If they want to get the kind of results you've gotten, they have to invest. Hire you for private mentoring, take an online course, buy this book. How do you monetize podcasting?

A: Glad you asked. My main company is Noise Media Networks. I market for clients with the goal of turning GMG into a million-dollar brand. If you're trying to make money from your podcast and you don't have many followers and downloads, you're not going to make a dime. In addition to consulting, I attached a t-shirt line and other products to my podcasts. I didn't want to fulfill orders. I designed items, added them in the store, and use my podcasts to promote and monetize. I'm creating a local brand and I've gotten my community involved. I also launched a comic strip for the t-shirts called Twinnemies. These twin sisters hate each other and don't know they're siblings. The comic strip has been getting lots of positive feedback. I also printed slogans from my town, 'Better Together' and 'Success Lives Here' on shirts. Podcasting has opened lots of doors that way.

V: What platform do you use for the merchandising?

A: <u>Printful.com</u>.

V: You set-up the account and they fulfil orders. No on-hand inventory. Good stuff. Some hosts have tried sponsors and advertisers, others charge experts to be guests on the show. I don't like that model. What about licensing? Has anyone tried to license your show to air in another market?

A I spoke at PodFest 2019. A woman approached me about licensing my content for their network. I didn't like their terms. It was a huge network that wanted me because I'm a Black woman. They needed diversity because their sponsors asked for it. Not many of us are out there. Of about two million podcasts, probably three percent are Black owned. The space is wide open. My goal for Noise Media is to build it into a network of shows, apps, and network partners. Keeping my content in-house and under my brand is essential to build a legacy business for my daughter and granddaughter.

V: I published a book with my granddaughters, *Oh, The Things I Can Be When I See Me*. I wanted them to know they could be whatever they want to be with examples of women of color who have done what they hope to do and look like them.

I googled 'how to podcast' and 975 million results returned in less than a second. Anchor, BuzzSprout.com, and Kajabi.com were at the top of the list of paid ads. What platform do you recommend to produce and distribute podcasts and why?

A: That depends on you as the host. I use Spreaker.com because I have a call-in show. Spreaker and BuzzSprout are very podcaster friendly. If you're not doing call-ins and you need customer service to get back to you immediately, use BuzzSprout. When Anchor first came out, everybody was excited because you just popped out your phone to go live. You can add intros and outros from the app. Spotify bought Anchor. Hosts are hopeful that the change will help build their podcast brand.

You have to know which platform is better for you. Spreaker works for me because it allows unlimited podcasts and guests can listen live from my website. <u>Blubrry.com</u> is a good platform that allows you to build a network. <u>Libsyn.com</u>, Blubrry, and <u>BlogTalkRadio.com</u> are the granddaddies in this space. I pay $50 a month and I have five podcasts on my platform. With BuzzSprout, you're going to pay $12 per podcast. You have unlimited downloads, but you're paying per podcast.

V: Do the episodes take up memory on your website?

A: They do not because it's embedded from Spreaker. I plop the link onto my website and send GMG listeners there. Spreaker distributes my podcasts to Apple podcasts, Google podcasts, Spotify, SoundCloud, iHeart, Deezer, a Chinese company called Giovan, Facebook, YouTube, and Twitter.

V: All for $50 a month. It's worth the investment.

A: Valerie, the only time I do anything with my podcast is on Thursday when I download it to add to my TV network. The only place they don't distribute to is Instagram, so I use <u>Headliner.app</u> for that.

V: Downloads and listens measure the reach of a show. What other indicators determine the success of a show?

A: What makes a show successful is if people come back to listen to you. Brands want to know how many repeat listeners you have and how many of them interact with you. If your goal is to build a podcast to get brands to support your show, it's going to take time. That's why I'm a believer of creating your own brand and selling your own product. You can lose your mind trying to get your numbers up.

You may have a following of a hundred people who are engaged and love you. That's successful. People call, text, and email me about how much they love the show. I often run into listeners who tell me that they love the music, commentary, and guests. A young lady in New York called me to schedule a consultation session. Success is based on you and your intentions for the podcast.

V: Absolutely. I compiled an anthology, *The Wait of Success: How to Become an Overnight Success in 7300 Days*. Success to me, may not be success to you. You named success on your terms, which minimizes comparisons with other shows.

A: Valerie, did you know Amazon does live streaming (Amazon.com/Live)?

V: I did not.

A: One of my friends in Gwinnett has a show called *Dealcasters*. He brought me on as a guest to talk about my podcast and what microphones I use. He put my books in a virtual carousel. As he interviewed, my books and preferred microphones were displayed for the audience to purchase. Over eight thousand people watched the interview! I woke up to deposits from Amazon.

If you could get approved as an Amazon Affiliate (Affiliate-Program.Amazon.com), you and the authors you interview can make money. You can use a similar technique with StreamYard.com. Create a package for authors with StreamYard interviews and product displays.

V: I use StreamYard. That's a monetizing nugget.

A: Amazon is the best live streaming platform on the planet. On Facebook Live, you may see two, twenty, or forty people. But one hour on Amazon Live, and thousands of people listened to me.

V: That's good. I want to talk more about music. I have a producer who creates original theme songs branded with my name, business, and books. When I host interviews, I play a theme song as the intro to give people time to log in and as the outro. Where do you get licensed music for your show?

A: I use Epidemic Sound (EpidemicSound.com) because Spreaker has a partnership with them. It's $99 a year to use as much music as you want. I also use Pond5.com. If I want an original song, I go to Fiverr.com. I'm about to get a jingle made for Gwinnett County. It's going to be the county's theme song like Frank Sinatra did for New York. I'm getting a theme song to build my brand. You pay the provider and Fiverr gives you commercial rights.

V: Music is a conduit that sets the mood and encourages creativity. What is the biggest marketing challenge for authors and how do you serve them to overcome it?

A: The biggest marketing challenge for most authors is introducing themselves to the right people. They're artists who prefer to stay behind the pen where they are comfortable. You have to get on the other side of the mic and in front of the TV camera. I can create and share your book trailer on my network. For $99, it lives on Roku forever. Nike never says, "Buy Nike." They play the commercial, and people who want to be associated with the brand buy it. They're building brand awareness and that's what authors should do. Think about their books as a brand under their umbrella company. Each book is a different brand that requires a different marketing plan. Yes, you may have to pay a few dollars, but it's worth it to be on TV.

V: It's advertising. I've seen people charging a hundred dollars to be a guest on their Facebook Live. I have been on ABC, NBC, CBS, Fox, Public Access TV, and a local high school channel for free. Why would I spend a hundred dollars for twenty fans?

A: Think about this, Valerie. You're a big dog with puppies who can't get on NBC and CBS yet. They may have to pay to get twenty views.

V: Good point. I work to position my clients to get TV ops and newspaper articles. It's about putting the pieces together so it makes sense for the journalist, reporter, or producer who needs content.

A: And we do not want something that we have to edit. We want it ready so we can just drop it.

V: That's true for just about anybody in business. I want to work with people who are teachable, willing to learn, and do the work. I mentor and guide them through what they need to do with checklists, templates, and other resources. Last question. What is your favorite resource and why?

A: Artificial intelligence. I want my network to run 24/7. I can't do that myself, but I can program it. On a Sunday, I can upload fifty-two episodes to run weekly. It's my content, my voice. I'm excited about the doors that opened because of this technology.

V: Audrey, chief noisemaker, thank you so much for sharing all this information about podcasting.

A: Thank you for having me. It's good to be on the other side of the mic. You have to come on GMG.

V: Absolutely!

Audrey Bell-Kearney is a diehard entrepreneur with more than twenty years of experience. She invented the first plus-size fashion dolls, authored five books, and loves helping people realize their dreams. She hosts Good Morning Gwinnett (GMG) Podcast Monday through Thursday live at 10 AM EST. GMG is a hyperlocal hybrid podcast spotlighting people and places of Gwinnett County, GA and beyond. She launched Podcast University to help entrepreneurs learn how to leverage podcasting to create more awareness for their brand.

Connect with Audrey
NoiseMedia.us
Amazon.com/author/audreybellkearney
Facebook.com/GoodMorningGwinnett
Instagram.com/GoodMorningGwinnett

Audrey's Favorite Resource
Artificial intelligence because it allows her to create content faster.

Landing Deals with Traditional Publishing Houses

Vanessa Miller Pierce

V: Joining me today is multi-bestselling author and founder of Christian Book Lovers Retreat, Vanessa Miller Pierce. Vanessa is a natural-born writer who has written fifty novels. Several of them landed on *Essence Magazine's Bestsellers List.*

She creates characters facing multi-dimensional struggles to drive home the message of redemption. I met Vanessa at Revival Center Ministries in 1994. We worked together on plays where she directed and I acted, and a conference for singles. At the launch party for her first book, *Former Rain*, which was self-published, Nessa asked Rhonda and me to partner with her with Butterfly Press. My job was all the left-brain stuff: taxes, logistics, inventory.

Nessa, I had to have you in this project because you have done something most indie or self-published authors only dream about doing. You landed publishing deals with five different real traditional publishers. And I said "real" because I see people on Facebook claiming to be a traditional publisher. The devil is a lie.

As a self-published author, you sold tens of thousands of copies of one title. You had four titles before you landed a deal with a traditional publisher. Who was your first publisher?

N: My first traditional publisher was Urban Christian. They were an imprint of Kensington, which provided the distribution.

V: How did you land that deal? I know that's a loaded question.

N: The first deal was with Joylynn Ross. I am so thankful to her. We often ran into each other at book signings. When she became the editor at Urban Christian, she contacted me. She said, "Vanessa, would you like to bring your *Rain Series* to Urban Christian?"

I felt like I lived in hotels. I owned a home, but I felt like a visitor there because I traveled so much to get the word out about my books. When she contacted me, I was ready to say, "Yes!" I needed help. Urban Christian accepted *Former Rain, Abundant Rain,* and *Latter Rain.* Even though they had already been published and sold tens of thousands of copies, they re-published them. And then published *Rain Storm* and *Through the Storm* the fourth and fifth books in that series.

V: That is great. You mentioned lots of traveling. Many new authors try to do everything on social media. "I have a book. Buy my book." As we know, that strategy doesn't often work. One strategy you used was military bases. How was that for you?

N: My first book came out in 2003 when not as many authors were signing at military bases. It was a beautiful thing. I was able to cover all my travel expenses and make a profit.

Some readers introduced me to family and other readers who weren't in the military. I often went to the military base in Maryland and started meeting with book clubs there. They were the first book clubs to register for the Christian Book Lovers Retreat (CBLR). People are probably tired of me saying how much I love Maryland, but they don't understand how good Maryland has been to me.

V: Relationships are powerful. I met one of your avid readers at your wedding. I sat next to her and her daughter.

N: I met Minister Jacquelyn Arnold at a Maryland military base almost twenty years ago. That woman is so special to me. Not only did she buy all of my books, she visited me at the base. She invited me to speak at the church she attended. They bought tons of books.

She always looks out for me. In *Through the Storm,* I wrote about the prayer journey we did at Revival Center years ago. After reading the book, people contacted me to do the journey. I'm not that tactical person who writes out every step. Minister Jacquelyn had built an entire prayer journey and held them at her church. When I told her that people were requesting information from me, she gave me pages and pages of her content.

In 2018, she came to the retreat at Myrtle Beach and hosted the prayer journey. When I ask her for something, she's there. And when she asks me for anything, I'm like, "What do you need?"

V: You developed and nurtured that relationship so that it was reciprocal. If you treat this book business as a transaction, you got a one-time sell. But if you nurture relationships, you have lifelong friends.

Nessa, how did starting as a self-published or independent author help you land that deal?

N: Joylynn saw me hustling. You have to keep going. You keep praying about what you want, believe, and trust that God is going to work out things for you. God has already given you the things that you need to succeed, but you have to work it out. You can be out doing what you do and then boom! Something wonderful happens organically. It's not necessarily anything you plan. I'm releasing two books, *Dreams Come True* and *Once Upon a Dream* for my publisher, Whitaker House. I changed the titles, updated the books, and did different things to them. I just received an email from *Women's World Magazine. Once Upon a Dream* was selected to be featured in their July 2022 issue. It will be at newsstands, grocery stores, and more the last week of June. That's nothing I planned. I asked how they found the book. She said that they scour different places looking for books they can promote and found mine on Amazon.

V: What is their reach? Do you know how many women they have as subscribers?

N: Oh, it's got to be quite a bit. Readers don't have to be subscribers because *Women's World* is in grocery stores. Blessings like that happen as you do your daily duty. But you have to be out there. You have to be doing. I could have decided not to re-publish it. I think the new cover caught her eye. As a self-published author, you want to make sure that you're producing good covers. You don't know if people are looking to advertise you based on how nice your book cover is.

She went to my website, so she knew I was a Christian fiction author. I don't think they only promote Christian fiction, but for this issue, that's what they wanted.

V: You were ready. Like the five wise virgins, you had your oil lamp full. She visited your website and checked you out. People do all kinds of research on you. If all they find is your Facebook page with you doing booty posts and flashing dollar bills, that's not going to win them over. Your social media page may not really give as much intimate or personal information about you, but you can put your bio on there. So, she went to your website, saw your other books, and CBLR info. Authors, Facebook is not your website. Have a website with your name as the URL, which is another great tool. Don't do fancy names. I know people who misspelled their name—

N: Wait a minute. Why do they want to spell it differently?

V: "It makes me unique." Yeah, so unique that readers can't find you. Combining letters and numbers to spell names. Awful. In real-life, grinding made you visible selling books. Traditional publishers want to know that you are going to be viable and valuable. Because they invest money, time, and risk. They're editing, printing, distributing, and marketing. They're incurring all the risks and want to make sure that they're going to get back their money. You showed that you're going to do the work to get their money and yours.

N: Exactly. One of my current publishers, Thomas Nelson, which is part of Harper Collins, asked me to do a video for their sales team. If the salespeople are selling your book, that's going to help your book do well in bookstores. When I did the video, I made sure to tell them my goal for my new book, *Something Good,* which releases March 2022, is to make the *USA Today Bestseller List.*

I don't keep that goal to myself. Every time I talk to them, I restate my goal. If it doesn't happen, it doesn't happen, but I'm going to work hard to get there. So, when I did the video for the sales team, I said, "My goal for *Something Good* is *USA Today*

Bestseller List. Not only are you guys working hard to make that happen…" I know they're going to work hard because that's what they do. I told them the things that I'm going to do on my end to promote the book.

I think many authors feel like once they get a publisher, they don't have to do anything. Incorrect. The publisher can get your book into bookstores and get lots of publicity for your book; however, the author must bring something to the table. You don't know how much your efforts will add to what they do. It is possible to sell more books than a person who makes *USA Today* or *New York Times*, but sales didn't hit at the needed time. Don't be misled. Authors may reach those bestseller lists, but another author in the house may be selling more books than any of them. Publishers love those authors.

V: That makes sense. Because it takes a specific strategy to hit those lists. If you sell a bunch of books out the back of your car, or you're selling through distributors that don't report sales, you could be making a bunch of money and still miss the list. The good thing about hitting a popular list is that you have national and possibly international visibility. More people learn about you and your books. I cyber touch and agree with you that you hit *USA Today*.

N: Amen. I have never had a goal like that before. I always wanted to write at least a hundred books before I'm done, and I am in the second half of my career. Of course, if the Lord wants me to write more than a hundred, I'm here for it. I decided that I want to make the *USA Today Bestseller List* and I'm going for it.

V: Things that helped you transition from self-published to land the first traditional deal were the fact that you were busy and getting trackable results. You built your platform, so you were an easy win to them. This opportunity is a no-brainer; we need to move with her. Let's talk about some of the major differences between traditional and self-publishing.

N: A major difference is that a traditional publisher can get your book in bookstores much easier than you can as a self-published author. I am not that thirty-year-old newbie. I don't have the time and energy I did back then.

V: You were everywhere. Your books were in bookstores, libraries, and the streets of New York with authorized vendors.

N: Right. I didn't have grandkids then and I wasn't married. What are you willing to give up as a self-published author to ensure success? I decided that I wasn't willing to give up everything.

V: I know that's right. You must have life balance.

N: I'm thankful because being traditionally published helped me when Amazon launched Kindle. It was a stressful time for me as my mom had just passed.

I had missed a deadline on one of my books with a publisher. And I don't miss deadlines. I'm the one who turns manuscripts in early because I want to be thought of as a professional.

V: Easy to work with.

N: Yes. After my mom passed, I was supposed to do a sequel to *How Sweet the Sound*. I had nothing in me and couldn't write the sequel. So, I started writing novellas, which were easier for me. Because I had such a difficult time praising God after I lost my mother, I wrote a series called *Praise Him Anyhow*. That series took off on Kindle. Series tend to sell well for self-published books, but I wasn't doing anything to promote. The timing was right because people were getting Kindles and wanted eBooks. They loved the series and wanted more. I felt like I could do this again.

Self-publishing wasn't difficult in the beginning. What became a struggle was when my first publisher wanted to pay me once or twice a year. When the check was short or they messed up royalties, they told me, "Pray about it, and hopefully, you'll get it the next time." I'm not praying about my money. Just give it to me.

V: If I have to find a fish on the riverbank to eat...I need my money.

N: Right. At a time when my career should have been growing, it was halted. From the outside, my books were in lots of stores, and making the

Essence Bestseller List, but it was one of the worst times in my life as far as my career.

V: When you're writing your novellas, you do those as a hybrid model. You created the novellas as eBooks, is that correct?

N: Yes. Eventually, I let Amazon print them because I had people who only read physical books. I felt like I was early on Kindle when I started publishing my novellas. It was easy and I made more doing that than I ever made with my publisher.

V: Sitting at home collecting checks every month.

N: I was happy. Authors need to understand that you have to stay up on technology. I wasn't doing much marketing. I wrote it and they came. I was still going to book club meetings. Military bases started not to be as effective. Know that there are different seasons for things. When a season ends, you have to understand the next season. I put out a book and debuted as the number one bestseller in my category. It organically happened. Then I noticed a shift. My titles weren't making the top 10 or top 20. And I'm like, "What's going on?" I had gotten so excited about the Christian Book Lovers Retreat that I didn't realize my readers weren't finding my books. I knew I needed to do something different because there's so much noise out there.

I went to my agent and said, "I want to come back to traditional publishing. Do you think there's a house for me?" She said, "Let's try it and see." I submitted a proposal that I had written years ago because I was so busy. She sent it out and we got rejection after rejection. Keep in mind, I was used to publishers loving my work.

One editor, Jocelyn Bailey at Thomas Nelson, had *Hallelujah Anyhow.* She did not reject it, but she hadn't accepted it either. I'm going into inspirational women's fiction where many of my books have been romantic. She purchased and read *Long Time Coming.* She told me that she liked that book, but didn't like my proposal for the new book.

I wrote a new proposal. I knew that it had to be the best proposal I ever wrote especially since I was trying to come back into traditional publishing after being gone for many years.

V: You had to rebuild yourself.

N: And things changed. I wrote the proposal for *Something Good* and prayed like never before. "Lord, give me an idea." I felt like many of my author friends came up with awesome ideas. But when I came up with the proposal for *Something Good,* I knew it was a winner. Even the title told me it was something good. My agent liked it and sent it back to Jocelyn. Within a week, they emailed me. I met with the publisher by video chat due to COVID. They wanted to talk to me to make sure I was the right fit for Thomas Nelson. They want you to be visible and care about your readers.

V: And love what you write. Not writing because it's the next best thing, but because that's your lifestyle.

N: Right. Passionate about what you're writing. It was a good talk and then we got the contract. As I've told authors whose proposals bounced around without results, maybe that's not the proposal for this time. Submit something else if that one is not working. But so often, we get stuck on a story because we like it and assume everyone else will like it, too.

They may not like it because they bought a similar story from a different author. The rejection may not necessarily be about you as the author. The publishing house determines how your story fits their model. You can't be mad that other people land deals when you're not willing to try something else.

V: You mentioned proposal. When you submitted the proposal, was the book already written or did you write the book after it was bought?

N: I don't write a book without a contract if I'm writing for a traditional publisher. If you don't have many books out or you're a first-time author, the publisher will want the completed book. But if you have many books, the publisher may request the first two or three chapters and an outline. If they like the chapters and outline, then a contract will be written with a timeline for when the full book is required.

V: That's good for authors to know. A team of people are evaluating and making decisions on how you fit. They aren't looking for a one-hit wonder. They are looking for connection and ongoing relationship. Many authors who are trying to shift from self-publishing to traditional don't understand that they need to be avid writers with a cache or queue of ideas and books. If they want to sign you for a four-book deal, you better be able to write four books.

N: Yes, yes. And when you come from self-publishing, you want to market those books because a traditional publisher will ask for your numbers, so they know what you bring. They already have a customer base so they want to know what you can deliver. You need to be able to show how many copies you sold of each book.

V: And they need to be proven numbers because anybody can make up numbers.

N: You can go pull numbers from Amazon and Barnes and Noble. I spent a whole weekend getting my numbers.

V: But it was worth it.

N: Right. I didn't just pull numbers out of the sky. If sales aren't that good, don't worry. If the proposal is great, the publisher may be less concerned about sales, especially if you're a first-time author. Work on making that proposal something they can't say no to.

V: You said something earlier that leads back to integrity. The fact that you make sure that you submit books, not on time, but early. You also indicated that as a traditionally published author, you invest in editing.

By the time you send it to the house, it's clean. It may not be ready to go, but you didn't send them subpar just to make the deadline. Because of your work ethic and integrity, it made it easy for them to see you as a good fit. And here's proof; receipts like young people say. Authors saying that they sold out of books isn't saying much. If you only brought ten books, selling out is not a big deal.

N: Right. Authors don't get that you have to hustle to sell those books. Like I said, it was much easier years ago. Now, there's so much competition. You need to be on Instagram. You need to sell books on Twitter. I still don't understand that one. Facebook used to be good. You had thousands of people on your pages, but...

V: Everybody doesn't see your posts because they limit how many people can see it. That's why I tell my clients to send people to your website. You need to connect with them on a more intimate level, get their email, and stay in touch. Algorithms can change at any time. The new thing comes and you're trying to build a new tribe. I claimed @penofthewriter on Clubhouse, but I can't manage all this effectively.

N: I'm on Clubhouse, but I don't have time to go there. I don't understand where people get all of this time.

V: A question I often get from clients is how do you price eBooks? When it comes to pricing print books, you evaluate your costs and competition comparing page count, book format, and several more factors. Pricing eBooks is different. I've seen people charge $9.99 for the eBook, when the print version is $14.99. Some pick numbers out of, as my coach says, "Their who-ha." It makes no sense, no rhyme or reason. What's your eBook pricing strategy?

N: Lots of traditional publishers charge $9.99 or higher for eBooks and they can. Readers who love an author, will buy the book. I think people perceive those books as better quality because of the editors and staff.

If it's a novella, I charge $3.99, but if it's a full novel, then I charge $4.99 or $5.99. Of course, the publisher is going to be higher because of the middleman. They have to pay me. They have to pay the online people. They have to pay the people who work at the publishing company, so the book costs more coming from the publisher. The book that I have coming out with Thomas Nelson next year is 97,000 words. I have never written a 97,000-word book. That's almost two books for me.

I want to transition to women's fiction which is typically 80,000 to 120,000 words. That's another reason why an eBook is $9.99. A self-published eBook that's 60,000 words may go for $4.99 or $5.99. Now you're getting almost a hundred-thousand words.

V: That's why I said that you are a natural-born writer. Eleven years later, readers still ask me for the sequel to *The Forbidden Secrets of the Goody Box*. I can't get in the creative space to write because I'm busy doing work for clients. You definitely have a clear space to write. You've done hybrid publishing. You have traditional deals and you're self-publishing novellas and eBooks. Quite a few traditional authors are shifting away from traditional publishing and moving into self-published arenas. Why do you think that shift is happening?

N: Authors finally figured out that they can make money without the traditional publishers. With self-publishing, my books were not necessarily in bookstores unless I did a signing. But because of the traditional publishing deals, people came looking for my self-published titles. I had such a hard time, especially with my first publishing deal, but I'm grateful for the experience.

I learned a lot and the books were in lots of places. Still today, people tell me that they read one of my books from that first deal. That's how I ended up with the readers that I have. I'm thankful. When I went back to self-publishing, the readers followed me. They found me from so many different ways.

You have to be grateful for whatever state you're in and recognize that God is working out something for your good. You may not see it at that moment but sit back and wait. You are going to be blessed out of your socks.

Keep doing the work. Trouble won't last always. Keep doing what you're doing and keep believing. I was born to write. This is a job I would do if nobody paid me. Even through the lean years, I kept working. Because it's in me, I can't help but write. I have stories that are meant to touch the heart and soul of my readers. I have stories that are meant to bring people back to God or give them a better understanding of His forgiving power, His love, and His grace for whatever they have going on. As long as people buy my books, I intend to keep writing. I love what I do.

V: You entertain, but you also embed powerful messages. I think that's the connection. Not only are you entertaining with the storyline and characters, you're also teaching life lessons. Like with *The Goody Box Book*, I'm sure you had readers say, "This book changed my life." How can you not operate in your gift when you get those kinds of responses?

Even when the money is low, we know God is faithful. We worked together on the *Abundant Rain* stage play. You've published anthologies launching careers for other authors, and then you have the Christian Book Lovers Retreat. You expanded beyond the book, which is important for authors to understand. Don't just think about the book because it can go so much bigger. Tell me about CBLR.

N: We're doing one virtually for authors this year. We're bringing editors from traditional publishing houses so they can pitch their story. As I get older, I'm always thinking about the younger Vanessa who wants to do this for God. We also do an annual in-person retreat that started in 2016. Before my ankle was broken in a car accident, I traveled to book club meetings and events. After the accident, I couldn't travel. I had to learn how to walk again because somebody was distracted by a dropped cell phone, swerved into oncoming traffic, and hit me head on. Praise God, I'm still here! I moped around the house because I couldn't go anywhere. My daughter said, "Why don't you bring them here? People like Charlotte." I never considered it until she said that. I went to my Facebook group and asked my readers if they would come to a retreat. The response was great. Then I asked what they wanted to experience, and we started planning. Authors came to me volunteering to help so, we developed a board. This happened in four months! Over a hundred people attended the first one. This year, we were expecting 500 guests, but we're only accepting about half that for social distancing.

V: I have spoken at several of the retreats about *The Goody Box Book* and book publishing. I missed the first year because I had a prior obligation. It's a powerful retreat. You feed guests. You entertain them. You minister to them, and they get to meet authors at a mass book fair. It was a great experience for authors, presenters, and readers. Not only do you talk about Christian living and lifestyle, but general self-care practices for women. I'm an introvert, I don't go to all those parties. I speak, and then go to my room because I need to rest and recover. I can't do the parties. Too sensory for me.

N: Girl, we have fun.

V: I speak, eat, and go to my room to sleep. I highly recommend CBLR. If you're an author or a reader who loves Christian clean, inspirational entertainment and fun, you need to be at the ChristianBookLoversRetreat.com.

Nessa, what is your favorite resource and why?

N: My journal because I'm always writing and my planning calendar. I write what's scheduled for the week and then I look over it because I will forget that I'm scheduled for something. I have learned to write everything and then review it every morning as a reminder.

V: It helps you stay organized and declutters your brain. Because if you're trying to remember too much stuff, you can't be creative to write. And you forget things. So, it's good to put it in writing. Write the vision and make it plain.

N: I used to not use a planning calendar because my schedule was in Google, which sends email reminders. But if I leave the house, the pop-up reminders don't help me. So, I refer to the written schedule. And I now have a virtual assistant (VA) because I can't do it all.

V: Those are good organizational tools. You have deadlines and books to write, so you let your VA focus on building the email list and admin stuff. My VA is in the Philippines. She manages my social media posts. Even when I'm out of town or busy, something is posting on social media. Sometimes I share them to my writing group.

N: People don't understand how much work it is. You have to figure out what you can do and what can you delegate. And what you can do to remind yourself of what you are supposed to do.

V: I set multiple reminders. My Google calendar alerts me the day before and an hour before a task. My scheduling app sends two reminders (https://acuity.jnqsge.net/zaa2RW). I set my phone to remind me fifteen minutes before an interview, so I'm online and ready. With so many distractions, I don't want experts waiting for me to apply makeup.

Nessa, thank you so much. You shared a wealth of information. I am excited for aspiring authors to understand the process of landing, not one, not two, but five deals with traditional publishing houses. I'll have you on next time to talk about how to get an agent and deal with acquisition editors.

Connect with Vanessa. Once you jump into a series, you're going to want more. Here's to an abundant event for the Christian Book Lovers Retreat, the virtual retreat for authors, and all the other stuff you're doing. I speak God's blessings on your enlarged territory. Lord, keep giving her witty inventions and new ideas.

N: Amen.

Vanessa Miller Pierce is a best-selling author, playwright, and motivational speaker. As a child, she spent countless hours reading and writing. Vanessa's creative endeavors took on new meaning when she became a Christian. Since then, her writing deals with redemption, often focusing on characters facing multi-dimensional struggles. She is an ordained minister, explaining, "God called me to minister to readers to help them rediscover their place with the Lord."

In 2016, Vanessa launched the Christian Book Lovers Retreat to bring readers and authors of Christian fiction together in an environment of faith, fun and fellowship.

Connect with Vanessa
VanessaMiller.com
Facebook.com/VanessaMiller01
LinkedIn.com/in/vanessa-miller-55a5b810
Twitter.com/VanessaMiller01

Vanessa's Favorite Resource
A journal for writing and capturing her planning calendar.

Millionaire Math with the 5Cs

Brother Bedford

V: Joining me today is revered marketing and business advisor to entrepreneurs, specifically Black entrepreneurs, Brother Bedford. He is founder of the Masters of Business Network and Mastermind Community, and he hosts Conversations with Black Millionaires Podcast, which is named from his book of the same title. He co-hosts POWER Podcast with business icon, Dr. George C. Fraser. As a result of his first book, he has shared the stage with sports stars, celebrities, and legendary entrepreneurs including Les Brown, Dr. Dennis Kimbro, and Lisa Nichols.

For those who don't know your backstory, tell us how you leveraged the expertise of others to build your brand.

B: Thank you so much, Valerie, for inviting me to be part of this project. I'm honored because of the work that you do. I know how hard you work to help people get their voices heard and take their ideas from pen to paper. I'm excited and honored that you asked me to be a part.

As it relates to my story, I was born and raised on the east side of Detroit. I started as an entrepreneur in the entertainment space doing concert promotions. Then I stumbled into information marketing, what we now call knowledge-based or self-education industry, a little over twenty years ago. Since the pandemic forced people to go inside to use their knowledge and expertise to create products, digital products and books, the industry is approaching a billion dollars a day.

I started creating digital reports and sold them online for $7. I read a book called *Conversations with Millionaires,* and I noticed that the book only had one Black person in it, Wallace Amos from Famous Amos Cookies. That's when the idea hit. I said, "Wouldn't it be nice if someone interviewed successful Black millionaires and put that in an eBook?" I was reading two books at that time: *Success Runs in Our Race* by Dr. George C. Fraser and *Think and Grow Rich, A Black Choice,* which Dr. Dennis Kimbro co-wrote with Napoleon Hill. They were the first two people I called.

I called to Cleveland, Ohio. A young lady answered the phone. I said, "Hi, this is knucklehead Brother Bedford from Detroit. I have this idea to interview successful Black millionaires, and I'd love to interview Dr. Fraser. She said, "I don't think he would be interested."

Because I wasn't CNN, *New York Times,* or a major publication calling for an interview, she didn't think Dr. Fraser would be interested. My little ego was crushed, but I was persistent. "Tell you what, I'll leave my number and if Dr. Fraser is interested, maybe he can give me a call to do the interview." She said, "Why don't you leave your number and call back in six months?" I hung up the phone deflated. But around five minutes later, my phone rang. I heard airport noise in the background. Dr. Fraser said, "Young man, this is George Fraser. I hear that you want to interview me." I put down the phone and covered it. My heart was beating. I said, "Yes, sir, Mr. Fraser, I do want to interview you, but I can't do it this way. Please call into my bridge line." He called my FreeConferenceCall.com number and we did the interview. We talked for about an hour and forty-five minutes.

I had the interview transcribed and that was chapter one of the eBook. I called to Atlanta for Dr. Dennis Kimbro. His assistant said the same thing about him not being interested. Lo and behold, about a week later, a deep, billowy voice called. "Young man, this is Dr. Dennis Kimbro. I hear that you want to interview me." I said, "Yes, sir!" I repeated the process using Fiverr.com. I sent the MP3 audio files, and they transcribed them. Now I had two chapters.

I strategically went after Dr. Fraser and Dr. Dennis Kimbro and then thought about how to leverage these experts to get other interviews. I called Les Brown's office…same thing happened, but here's the twist, Valerie. As I talked to Les Brown's assistant, she said, "Who have you interviewed already?" I said, "I've interviewed Dr. George C. Fraser and Dr. Dennis Kimbro." They were on the speaking circuit together, so it was to his advantage to say, "Sure, I'll do it." We had about a forty-minute conversation. We laughed like we were long-lost cousins. We had a connection. He's so energetic. Next, it was my favorite, Cathy Hughes. When I called her office, her assistant said, "Cathy answers her own emails. Why don't you email her?" When she replied to my email, she said, "Who have you interviewed already?" When I mentioned Dr. George Fraser, Dr. Dennis Kimbro, and Les Brown, she was interested. At the end of our discussion, I thanked Ms. Hughes for granting me the interview and highlight of my career. She said, "No, Brother Bedford, thank you for including me in it." Wait. Cathy Hughes thanked Brother Bedford. That's one of the greatest compliments I ever received.

Les Brown called me a "gold mine." I interviewed Michael V. Roberts and Lisa Nichols. I could go on and on with the list of people I interviewed. Many millionaires are busy, so I haven't been able to reach all of them. In fact, if Tyler Perry calls right now, I'll tell you that I have to go because Tyler Perry is on the line.

Feelers are always out there to interview people. No one told me no although one person asked for payment. Sometimes people ask me, "Do they pay for the interview or did you have to pay them?" No. The reason Dr. Fraser called me back, and what his assistant didn't understand, was entrepreneurs, thought leaders, published authors, or professors, want to get out their message.

I didn't realize it at the time, but I became media to them. I became a person who could introduce them to a new audience. They needed the exposure. What started as interviews formed into relationships. I helped George Fraser with online registrations for his Power Networking Conference. He invited me to speak, and I've been speaking at the conference for the past twelve years. When people see us together, they refer to me as "George's right-hand man, Brother Bedford." The power of interviewing millionaires blossomed into great relationships.

V: Powerful. Transference of credibility. You called yourself a knucklehead. I'm sure that's not how you introduced yourself to her. You felt a bit like an imposter?

B: Especially at the beginning. I wanted her to know that I knew that I was stepping into deep water with a bonehead idea. At that time, eBooks were not on Amazon. Once I finished the interviews, they were transcribed, converted to PDF form, and uploaded to my site. I sold the eBook using PayPal. Dial-up internet took forever, and the entire concept was foreign to a lot of people. I navigated to where people said, "Is he serious? Is this a real thing?" Eventually, people caught on and now it's commonplace.

V: Now, many people don't even buy print books anymore. Let's talk about the tribe you had in place. Many self-published authors tend to publish without a following; no tribe, no social media, nothing. Your book launched before social media, but you already had a tribe of people who had grown to know, like, and trust you. I heard you say that at one of the conferences we spoke at together. How did you build your tribe? They had to trust you to invest in you and this new digital book.

B: Absolutely. When I stumbled into this space, the first thing that we were told to do was build your email list. And as you mentioned, my focus has been Black entrepreneurs. I gave away a weekly newsletter and built my list that way. You're right. Before I introduced *Conversations with Black Millionaires*, I sold those $7 reports on real estate. The people on my list wanted to know how I created and sold the report, which was another eBook. I put my ideas to paper and sent an email with my PayPal link to purchase it.

I sent that email and avoided my computer like the plague the next day. I didn't want to open it because I didn't know if this would work. But when I opened my computer, I saw notification of payment received, notification of payment received...hundreds of them. I kept creating small digital products and built my list. My first brand was notification of payment received.

Before starting the interviews, I asked my list if they wanted to hear from successful Black millionaires. So, when I launched *Conversations*, they were waiting for it. That sent me on the journey.

V: That's amazing. I noted that you purchased <u>NotificationOfPaymentReceived.com</u>. Did I tell you that is brilliant to me? Anyone who has PayPal knows that when you get paid, they send an email with the subject line: Notification of Payment Received. People purchase domains grabbing other people's names. Hoping that when they get big, they have to buy the domain from them. You also have a course on that topic, which I took. A great course I learned digital content strategy from you. Do you still offer that course?

B: I give it away as part of the mastermind. That dovetails into strategies as a book author that create other revenue streams to consider before you even write the book. I used to say write your book and then think of these things. But now I tell people to think about the backend first. Your book becomes the platform that launches you into this new arena of generating income.

V: Like I ask my clients, "What is your ultimate objective because the book is just the start?" In engineering, we used to ask, "What does 'done' look like?" Because done is different for everybody. Not everybody wants to be a millionaire or build a massive platform.

I talked to an author who was going to have a national television appearance. She wanted me to redo her book in three weeks. Although I did not initially publish her book, I knew it needed more than three weeks' worth of work. When she said that she didn't want to be an author, I said, "If your objective is not to be an author, why are you spending time, energy, effort, and money on this book? If your plan is to use the book as a tool to leverage other aspects of what you're doing, then let's talk. Either way, it won't be ready at the end of the month."

B: Right, that's smart. Great, great advice.

V: I learned from Brother Bedford. We shared the stage several times at Red Ink Conferences. Each time you spoke, you shared powerful strategies. I've been doing this for quite a few years, but the first time I heard you speak, you went from presenting to making the offer. Seamless. I wish I had my recorder. Based on the offer you made and the number of people who responded, you made several thousand dollars in less than an hour. Powerful strategy. Part of this process is being a continual learner. You have to be teachable and willing to look at new ways, new options. I joined groups not necessarily for the content, but to learn from the tribe leader — their strategy, how they do what they do, and what tools they use to deliver content.

On another occasion, you did what I call millionaire math.

B: When someone wants to earn a million dollars, we lay out several ways to get to it, right?

V: Yeah. I love math, so I don't want to get too mathy, but you shared ways of generating multiple streams of income from one book. For those authors trying to hit six or seven figures, it's not likely going to happen with a $15 book. Selling a $15 book requires 66,667 books to hit a million. That number doesn't include publishing cost, so you probably have to sell 75-80,000 books to net a million dollars. Let's be very clear, we want that take home pay to be at least six figures.

Most self-published authors can't hit 250 books sold for many reasons. It's much easier to implement other strategies. Brother Bedford, let's go through that millionaire math by reviewing the number of people, the price of the product, and how the combination equates to a million dollars.

B: One of my students, Marquel Russell, sells only high-ticket items. Once you get into this industry, you learn what works best for you. A large percentage of people, we're talking maybe 95 to 98%, never sale more than 250 books for the lifetime of a book.

If you're not JK Rowling or the author of a mega book we've come to love, getting million-dollar book advances, you have to wrap your mind around it. The reality is doing those types of numbers, requires a whole lot of work. In terms of conversions, to sell 70,000 books, you have to reach well over 700,000 people to get a 10% conversion, which is pretty good. Most people function at a conversion rate of 1 to 3%. That's why you see people attempting to get lots of eyeballs on their products/services or drive traffic to their site. They need that volume of people to meet their income goals.

So how do you offset that volume? By offering higher-end products. It is wise to think about your book as your platform, calling card, or business card. It should be an introduction to who you are to create your platform and launch other products or services. The best way to do that is to reverse engineer other ideas.

You said it so beautifully about the client who wanted you to remake the book, but didn't want to be an author because I'm sure they realized it's not the most profitable business; however, your book creates so many other opportunities. Let's do the math. If you have a $200 product, you need 5,000 people to meet that million-dollar income goal.

V: So, 5,000 people times a $200 product will gross a million dollars.

B: Yes. I'll get to my sweet spot, which I love to tell people that they should consider. You need 2,000 people at $500, or 1,000 people at $1,000. And then you get into the higher-priced tickets that require fewer people to invest. A $2,000 product only needs 500 people. Think about that 10% conversion rate. You may already have 5,000 Facebook friends or Instagram followers.

If you have a different offering you're connecting or packaging with your book, you can see the potential or income that can be made. For 300 people, you need a product between $3,300 and $3,400, and 100 people for a $10,000 offering. I'm sure knees are shaking, asking, "Can I come up with a $10,000 product?" Absolutely, with the right mentoring. Valerie can help you come up with those types of products and services. You only need a hundred people to be a seven-figure income earner. Your book is a catalyst; however, if nobody knows, likes, or trust you; you don't have a platform or a message, that's what the book does. The book provides a platform, a way for you to offer services that could yield the type of revenue that most authors desire.

V: In a nutshell, the millionaire math is doable. You mentioned conversion rates. For people who aren't familiar with that term, what is conversion rate?

B: I'm glad you asked. No longer just think of yourself as an author. You have to think entrepreneurial; business minded, right? To be successful, you must incorporate the language. I think it was one of Robert Kiyosaki's books, where he explains the language that gets people rich. Knowing what to say and how to say it. Start incorporating the vocabulary of business to be in business.

Conversion rate means if a hundred people visit your website and ten people buy or sign up to do something like giving their name and email, then you have a 10% conversion rate, ten people out of a hundred took action.

In the world of online marketing, you can track analytics much better than a brick-and-mortar store trying to count the number of customers who entered the building and what they bought. Cumbersome, right? Too tedious and would probably drive entrepreneurs out of business. But in the online space, it's easy to track. If a hundred people came to my website and I sold 10 books, I have a 10% conversion rate, which is good. That business stat helps you with marketing. If you know that you have a 10% conversion rate, and you want to sell 100 books, you need to get a thousand people to your site. If you want to sell 1,000 books, you need to get 10,000 people to your site. That's how you do your numbers. You're not throwing spaghetti against the wall to see what sticks. You're intentional. When you know your numbers, you know how to better market. You know how to design your messaging and it becomes more controllable for you.

V: Shows like *Shark Tank* and *The Profit* delve into conversion rate, costs to attract a customer, and client retention costs. As you said, there's lots of business terms that we need to understand to be effective.

B: And if you noticed, when they don't know those numbers, they don't get the deal.

V: They sure don't. Beyond the book, what ways can authors establish a virtual empire?

B: That's a beautiful question. Not one person came through 2020 without Zoom, webinars, or some type of online training. We were doing this twenty years ago, but now people are more receptive to the concept. My concern about people using credit cards online, people do it willingly now. I want people to consider this model, which I call the 4Cs.

1. Classes
2. Courses fall into the $200 range. Sometimes they're a little cheaper due to market saturation.
3. Coaching is leading clients to understand their truth: self-discovery.
4. Consulting provides tools and resources for clients to execute the solution.

I advise authors to approach this model from one of two ways.

If you're going to be an author, approach it as a publishing company. Be prolific. Meaning you have a series of books that can yield passive income. Or, like what you do, Valerie, publish others or mentor them to DIY publishing. It's not one book, but 10, 20, 50 or more books.

A partner and dear friend, Ty Cohen, operates Kindle Cash Flow. He was an early pioneer of Amazon Kindle. Many of his students earn thousands of dollars a month by publishing eBooks. Here's the caveat: they're publishing hundreds of eBooks. Can you imagine if you had a hundred eBooks published and each book made $10 a day?

V: A thousand dollars a day is good passive income.

B: Thousands and thousands of books are being published. Scarcity isn't there to make people say, "Ooh, I have to get this book." Myriads of books on the same subject matter are available, so you have to know how to differentiate yourself, right? You can either publish lots of books for publishing revenue or you become the authority, which is where the term author derives. Be the authority or subject matter expert in an area that allows you to offer classes, courses, consultations, or coaching others through the process. If you are an expert in relationships, money, or health and wellness, you can provide valuable content and make money.

V: Lots of money. Please differentiate between a course and class.

B: Since the explosion of the online space, tons of people talk about creating courses. That's easier said than done. What I advise people to do is offer the class first, record it, and turn it into the course. No one tells you how much time it takes to create a course and make it sellable. It's not easy to create a course from scratch that people are going to buy. No one tells you the marketing dollars needed to convince people that you have their solution. Remember, people buy courses because they want a solution to a problem.

The experts don't tell you that creating a course takes hard work and lots of sales. Going back to conversion. Let's say you had a $200 course with the goal of generating a million dollars. You have to sell 5,000 courses, right? At a generous conversion rate of 10%, that means you have to get at least 50,000 people interested in your subject, and more importantly, if they are going to spend $200 or more with you, they have to know, like, and trust you.

I advise creating a class first. Get paid to offer a live four-week class that can be converted to a four-module course that's available online. That way you find out if people will pay for it, before investing time and money to create it. You get paid upfront to offer your class using Zoom. You can record it and use as-is for the course, or you can analyze the content to see what worked, what didn't work, what the students liked, what they didn't like, to create a better class. Present the revised class, get attendees to pay to participate, and create your course from the recording. Otherwise, you could end up with a lot of out-of-pocket expenses and time trying to create a course without knowing if you can even sell it. This way, you get paid to create the course by offering the class first.

V: That makes sense. Many people ask me the same questions or want to pick my brain for information. I'm not a zombie and I need all my brain food. To replicate myself and be more accessible, I'm working on a membership-style course, Pen of the Writer Academy. My intent with the academy is to guide aspiring and novice authors to write, publish, and market books. Like you said, it's a lot of work condensing two decades of experience into a one-year program. I have enough followers to make the program cost effective.

B: This is a great teachable moment. You said that you've been doing this for twenty plus years and you have a following. You have cache to know that you're going to have takers for this course. Most people who are just starting try to do what you're doing now. They don't have a following or cache.

Think about what Valerie said: how hard it is for her and the weight she's lifting to create this program. How much harder for someone who's just starting to offer a similar program without experience, resources, and fan base? Test the waters with a class to see if you have a viable product or service.

The online space does not come with guarantees. You have to develop your sea legs. It's completely different from driving on the street with straight lines and stop signs. You're out at sea and you have to navigate to find the North Star. The wind may take you off course and you have to be able to compensate to develop a good product or service. That's why you want to test the wind, test the waters, and find out what works.

One last secret: I did not know that *Conversations* would be such a hit. You may expect some products to be hits and they end up duds. Back to what you're putting together, Valerie. It's something you've been doing for twenty-plus years. It's your natural gift, second nature. You're downplaying it, but that may be what your audience needs. Always keep your audience first.

V: Absolutely. It is a very involved process. For people telling their life story, or sharing information with family and friends, I don't recommend authorship. Put your report together, go to the copy center, distribute it, and be done with it. You don't want to get consumed with the minutia and not generate revenue or results. That's the other thing, people jump into the 4Cs and don't have results yet.

B: Yes. And it takes time.

V: They haven't done anything for anyone, not even themselves. I am amazed at the questions and answers in social media groups. One person asked, "How do I work with the illustrator for my children's books? Do I tell him what size to do everything or do I let him decide?" Somebody commented, "You let him decide." What? If the illustrator dictates the parameters of the book, then it's not your book, it's theirs. You decide the book specs and then communicate it to your team.

It's scary when people jump into publishing and haven't experienced their own results. Like I tell my clients, "Don't chase the next hot topic. You can't chase the money."

B: That can be difficult in the online space because we're trained to do that. When you get into copywriting and online marketing, your job is to convince people that they need your service by any means necessary.

The fear of missing out (FOMO) is an element people put in their copy. It's important that you have to think of yourself as an entrepreneur. You're jumping on the other side of the fence. You have to be prepared to conduct your sales properly. You're right, there are lots of so-called experts who are giving so-called advice. I agree with you, nothing replaces investing in good, solid mentorship or courses from people you trust.

Don't be afraid to invest with the people who have done what it is that you want to do. You see the results of what they've done. You develop a relationship with them as a shortcut to your success. If you don't, you're going to be in for a long road.

I guarantee that person who took the advice to "let the illustrator decide," will waste the next six months to a year, frustrated about what the illustrator did. Or if the illustrator owns the work, the author will be limited to what they can do with their own book. When they could have just hired you, Valerie. Do not be afraid to write a check to somebody who can help shortcut your learning curve. What I just said is probably worth the entire training. If you find the right coach, trainer, or mentor, they will reduce your learning curve and get you to your destination faster.

V: Reduced time is money saved. Wasted time and money, like the person with the children's book. She pays this illustrator, and then tries to upload it to Amazon only to get an error message, "These files do not fit our parameters." The formatting is wrong. The wrong color scale was used. The illustrations are the wrong size. When you do it right the first time and connect with people who have already done what you hope to do, it makes a world of difference. Like you said, Brother Bedford, I hired four business mentors, you were one of them. Each one provided a unique niche to help me do things better and differently.

I hired my first mentor, Michael Dresser, to help me with interviews. I was doing tons of interviews, but not getting results. He helped me improve my interview skills, but the process was so entailed that I repurposed the training to create a signature speech for my novel, *The Forbidden Secrets of the Goody Box.*

I hired a mentor to help me develop a sponsor schedule, call script, and more to land sponsors for my live events.

And then business mentoring, you and Darnyelle Jervey Harmon helped me understand systems, principles, and the numbers behind doing what I do. If you're serious about being a successful author or entrepreneur, you have to understand the numbers. You said that you had an ultimate business model, did we hit that yet?

B: No. You mentioned the network and mastermind. I'm a firm believer that everyone should learn how to mastermind. Most people attribute that to Napoleon Hill. One of the principles in his book, *Think and Grow Rich*, was the principle of mastermind, which he learned from successful entrepreneurs and business owners, the wealthiest people on the planet, at that time. The principle of mastermind is that one mind gets with another mind and together they produce a new third mind that births new ideas and solutions. However, it didn't start with Napoleon Hill or JP Morgan. It is a biblical principal. "Where two or more are gathered, I am in the midst." [paraphrased Matthew 18:20 NKJV]

It's a universal principle that I believe is the ultimate business model of constructing a mastermind. I'm going to give it to you two ways. One is a business model. The other: if you're trying to learn how to be an entrepreneur, to learn from other people, it's best to join a mastermind. People used to ask me, "What is the one book I can read to learn entrepreneurism? Or what is the one course I can take?

V: One?

B: Right. There isn't one book. You just said that you hired four mentors. It's an immersive learning experience. The best way to master it is to join a mastermind with other likeminded individuals who are getting results. In a mastermind, people present their visions, goals, and objectives. They also share the challenges and obstacles that get in a way. The mastermind is a group of people giving you suggestions of things they've done to be successful to shortcut your learning curve. You don't have to read tons of books; you just pose a question to the group. If you want to expedite or accelerate your growth and learning, you want to find masterminds who are doing what you want to do.

On the flip side, how is this the ultimate business model? Because people pay premium prices to get in a mastermind with people who are getting results to learn from them. A bonus C to classes, courses, coaching, and consulting is community that's subscription or membership based. An interchangeable description includes group coaching; however, the difference in mastermind is not me teaching or telling everyone what to do. It's me facilitating to bring all the brilliance together. Group coaching is more of a push, whereas mastermind pulls more energy, more power into the circle to come up with brilliant ideas. They get feedback, guidance, and sometimes joint venture collaborations from people within the group.

The language may change depending upon the industry. For example, I have a client who deals with parents of children with ADHD. In her situation, it's not a mastermind; it's a support group.

Here's what I found, Valerie. Masterminds accelerated my growth, but I never looked at it as a business model. Most people buy a course or coaching, but then the mastermind community accelerates your growth faster. People are writing big checks—$25,000, $50,000 a year— for this premium product. You meet in-person four times a year; however, since 2020 happened, people are doing it virtually via Zoom.

If you have a book and you're the authority on a subject, you can offer a community around that. It's so much easier than creating a course. People join the mastermind to access all of my trainings and courses. We have virtual office hours to conduct live sessions. We hold monthly masterminds where people are put on the hot seats. You may be thinking, "That seems like a lot." It is the easiest job I ever had. It is literally twenty hours a month—max. It takes an hour a week and three hours on Saturdays. When I'm creating new courses, I don't have to worry about creating a full curriculum. I create something, put it in the community, and it becomes a part of the ongoing training. We discuss it, so I'm more of a facilitator versus a coach or consultant. I project that you're going to see more of this business model. It's been available as a high-ticket item, but more people are offering it like we do and as you mentioned, a membership. The difference: a membership has modules and you'll be coaching and teaching, whereas mastermind people bring their energy, expertise, and knowledge to solve problems together. The ultimate business model.

V: Synergy, energy, and resources. Oftentimes, I get requests to find printers, editors, or illustrators. My community curriculum includes lists of resources. A partial list is available in the back of this anthology. It has elements of a mastermind, but I'm taking the lead. I'm anal about the quality of books. I'm very protective of the people in my circle, my tribe. A company reached out to me because they saw that I was getting things done. The rep said, "We'd like to send an email to your list and we'll pay you for it." Unimpressed with their money, I asked, "What information do you want to share to my list?"

Once he shared their objective, I said, "It conflicts with what I'm doing. Secondly, your prices are crazy. And I'm not doing that to my people."

Somebody who doesn't know any better will jump on this "deal" because I shared the email. Absolutely not. I didn't even ask him how much the company was going to pay me. It didn't matter. It wasn't worth me jeopardizing my integrity. I help my clients RISE with results, integrity, service, and excellence. One of my clients dubbed me the beautiful bully. She said, "Val is like a pit bull. Once she grabs hold to your vision, she won't let go."

B: I hope that everyone is picking up what you said. How many authors need to be what you've become? The protector of your tribe. Bringing valuable content and information that is beneficial. It's going to help with their future outcomes. That's the new business model.

Many of us have become transactional, buy this. It's slowly dying. I'll look into my crystal ball and say that, if you're struggling or stuck, it's probably because you're trying to sell something. But if you change the paradigm, and become more relational, then they know that you're protecting them and you're not bringing just anything to them.

Let's say you have fifty people like that. You offer enrollment in your mastermind for only a thousand dollars a year. You just made $50,000 and they know that it's going to be quality. That's how you start creating. From that, you can create a book.

V: Because they know you, they'll ask for your book. Not everybody can do the thousand dollars, but they can do a $15 book and tell other people about it. Another thing I've seen is affiliate programs. Hosting events and digital services, and then offering percentages to people who tell other people. You get your tribe—who already knows, likes, and trusts you—to pull in other people and make money for the referral. That's transference of credibility. "It worked for me. Give it a try, it'll work for you."

B: Yes. That means the person who has the attention and trust of an audience is the most valuable because affiliates are drawn to them. They want their offer to come through Valerie because she already cultivated an audience who would probably say yes to whatever Valerie recommends to them.

You have to think about yourself moving forward, when you're writing your book or creating content. Am I creating it for future outcomes of the people I want to serve? Here's the language I use for my mastermind: to whom do you want to be a hero or shero? Don't even write your book until you know who you want that book to be a hero to. If you want to be a shero to someone, who is that person? You're going to create a better product because you know what they need, what they want, what they need saving from. When you're a hero, individuals become endeared to you. They want to be around you. It goes back to being relational versus transactional.

For some reason, we want to get in and out of relationships like it's a bank robbery. But if this person brings me peace, value, or helped my bottom line, why would I want to break up that relationship? You want to do all you can to foster that relationship and continue to do business.

Relationship is important for authors because if you're just thinking of writing the book for yourself, you better write two books. Write the first one for yourself to get it out of your system, and then focus on who you want to serve.

V: That's what I do with my clients. Help them understand who they're writing to. What is your message to them? What problem are you fixing for them? In my mastermind, I'm creating a checklist to define an avatar of your ideal reader or client, so you can envision this person and understand what they want and need. Sometimes people don't know what they need until you tell them they need it.

You mentioned the sweet spot on the millionaire math. We didn't touch on that.

B: It's really simple. It's the one-thousand-dollar offer right in the middle. Most of us encounter a thousand people who would pay us for something. Your job and mine is to create, not necessarily a thousand-dollar product, but a thousand dollars' worth of value over the lifetime.

For people who say, "I can't create a-thousand-dollar product," find that customer and then make them a long-term customer who will pay you a thousand dollars over the lifetime. But if you want to get to it quickly, create a thousand-dollar product. Here's the thing about creating a higher-ticket product, it forces you to do your best stuff.

If you're going to sell a thousand-dollar product, you can't be skippy, or they won't buy it. You're going to dig deep. You're going to develop resources and checklists. The tools you put into your mastermind that anybody who's serious about being an author would say, "Val, I'll pay you a thousand dollars for that. That's less than ninety bucks a month. I can do that."

You can continuously feed them all this valuable information. So that sweet spot to millionaire is a thousand people and a thousand-dollar product. You can do it.

V: Sounds wonderful. One of your strategies is purchasing URLs for landing pages. It's much cheaper than having multiple websites and it helps people find exactly what you want them to find. Why do you use a unique URL for your landing pages?

B: Another great question. When all this stuff started, lots of people built bloated or billboard websites with bells and whistles. They found that people don't visit sites like that anymore. We call it the internet graveyard because these sites do not produce. It's like a brochure. What do people do with brochures? If they read and like it, they may keep it for reference or they throw it away. That's what those websites became. Landing or squeeze pages—called that because it's designed to squeeze information out of the person coming to the page—are more effective.

I have several URLs for different conversations depending upon where I'm speaking. When I gave marketing tips, I sent people to MoneyMakingMarketingTips.com to get my eight money-making tips. They went there for a specific purpose: to get the report, which was just a one sheet.

This is another lesson. It doesn't have to be a book. The tip sheet I gave away for free in exchange for their name and their email. They got relevant marketing tips. What did I have? The most important thing; they're on my list. Now I can develop and nurture the relationship with them, and then make an offer to sell. Most times, as you know, Valerie, my goal is to overwhelm them with value, so they eventually ask, "What is it that I can join? What can I buy from you?" You provide value in emails.

V: It's a great strategy. You get that ever elusive email, which is a powerful tool. Two more questions. What do you see as the biggest marketing challenge for authors and how do you serve them to overcome it?

B: The biggest marketing challenge is selling a book, especially if you're writing a long book like *Gone with the Wind*. That was one of the reasons I got away from courses. Statistics show, and I found this to be true, 98% of the people who invest in courses never complete them. And the stats are similar for books: 98% of the people will not read the entire book. People are bombarded with distractions that take away their time.

They really have to want your book to buy it. That's why I mentioned Ty Cohen earlier. His model is to sell short eBooks for $2, $3, but sell a whole bunch every day.

When people come to me, I tell them, "Don't write the book first. We need to create the back end and let the book come from there." Most of us have thousands of followers, but never asked them, "How can I help you?" That's one of the best lines to get your sales going. Scroll through your Rolodex and say, "I noticed that you were trying to write your book about two years ago. Have you written it?" If the reply is no, then you request to set up a phone call or Zoom meeting to "see how I can help you." You can find five to ten people in your phone right now who you can help and charge whatever, let's say $500. With ten people, you can make $5,000. Once you master the subject matter, you can write the book on what you did to get results for others; the solution that you provide.

V: And you're doing that through the mastermind community?

B: Yes. TheMobMastermind.com. MOB stands for Masters of Business.

V: Very good. Last question: what is your favorite resource and why?

B: To be able to pick up the phone, call George Fraser, and ask a question is priceless. You have to foster relationships to develop your own unique mastermind, so my favorite resource is the relationships I've built. If you ask me for a tool, my favorite is MightyNetworks.com. I use it to run my mastermind. I house courses and live stream through this platform. Everything I wanted to do for my mastermind I do in one place. I created a community so I don't have to have a separate Facebook group.

V: Great. Brother Bedford, every time we talk, I feel like a student because you have so much wisdom to share. It's important for people to understand that you weren't always Brother Bedford.

B: Absolutely. I'm glad you said that because that's the first thing you have to tell people: this journey was long and hard, but it can be done. Engaging, perfecting your craft, and meeting people like you, Valerie. Your Rolodex is thick, too. We know what you bring to the table. That's why people should connect with you. Not just transactional, but stay attached to Valerie to learn and grow with her. And it's reciprocal because as they're learning and growing with you, you're learning and growing with them. That's such a valuable way to look at relationships.

V: Reciprocity is powerful in all types of relationships: business and personal. No longer transactional, thank you. Thank you, Brother Bedford. I appreciate you so much.

Brother Bedford, founder of The Masters of Business Network & Mastermind Community, serves as one of the most trusted and revered marketing and business advisors to entrepreneurs and business owners. He hosts Conversations with Black Millionaires and co-hosts The Power Podcast with business icon, George Fraser. Brother Bedford has shared the stage with entertainers, sports stars, celebrities, and legendary entrepreneurs including George Fraser, Les Brown, Dr. Dennis Kimbro, Lisa Nichols, and Julianne Malveaux. Brother Bedford's life's work is dedicated to helping Black people grow businesses, advance careers, and expand their bottom lines exponentially.

<u>Connect with Brother Bedford</u>
BroBedford.com
Facebook.com/BroBedford1
LinkedIn.com/in/bro-bedford-a162a528
Twitter.com/BrotherBedford

<u>Brother Bedford's Favorite Resource</u>
<u>MightyNetworks.com</u>. He uses the platform to run his mastermind.

Celebrate Your Success

Valerie J. Lewis Coleman

We are serious about helping you land paid speaking engagements, media attention, and book sales. Contact me at info@penofthewriter.com with the book you published using *Do It Right the First Time* as your resource. Your book will be

- Included in an eblast to my 30,000+ fans, friends, and followers.
- Listed on the Pen of the Writer (POWER) Wall of Fame.
- Entered for the Do It Right Bestseller where the top-selling title will be acknowledged each year.

Plus, I'll host a live panel-style interview to further magnify and monetize your message.

I want to serve more aspiring authors to achieve their publishing dreams and I need your help. Can you do me a favor?

- Email me a testimonial about your experience with *Do It Right the First Time*. I'll share it on social media and my Google business page with a link to your site.
- Post on social media tagging me and the authors whose contributions helped you most. Use hashtags: #DoItRightTheFirstTime, #PenOfTheWriter, and #SelfPublishing to create a viral thread.

- Write an Amazon review at https://amzn.to/3zeQ51j. Remember, as Carolyn Howard-Johnson explained in our conversation, your reviews hyperlink back to your author page.

Congrats in advance!

Your Bestseller Resources

"I did then what I knew how to do. Now that
I know better, I do better."
—Maya Angelou

Marketing Resources

Talk with Val	https://penofthewriter.as.me
60 Minutes to Bestseller	Bit.ly/POWER60Mins (case sensitive)
Appointment Scheduler	https://acuity.jnqsge.net/zaa2RW (case sensitive)
CRM	HubSpot.com PipeDrive.com Save with promo code penofthewriter1851835
eCommerce	Paypal.com
File Sharing	DropBox.com WeTransfer.com
Headline Analyzer	AMInstitute.com/headline
Media	BlackGospelPromo.com BlackNews.com BlackPR.com Blavity.com HelpAReporter.com MadameNoire.com PRNewsWire.com RadioGuestList.com TheGrio.com TheRoot.com
Media Release	Email info@penofthewriter.com for samples of Pen of the Writer Releases
Online Calendars	AALBC.com/Events DaytonLit.com Writing.ShawsGuide.com

Online Presence	Author.Amazon.com Bit.ly Google.com/alerts GoodReads.com GoDaddy.com Moz.com/domain-analysis#index TinyURL.com
Mastermind Networks	MightyNetworks.com TheMobMastermind.com
Merchandise	Affiliate-Program.Amazon.com Printful.com
Reviews	BookFunnel.com ReadersFavorite.com
Royalty-Free Music	EpidemicSound.com Pond5.com
Podcasts	Amazon.com/Live Anchor.fm ArtistFirst.com Bit.ly/POWERStreamYard (case sensitive) BlogTalkRadio.com Blubrry.com BuzzSprout.com GetAudioGram.com Headliner.app Kajabi.com Libsyn.com Spreaker.com
Promote	Animoto.com Canva.com RoboDial.org Txt180.com/sl/22m

	VistaPrint.com WheelOfNames.com
Promoters	LaShaundaHoffman.com SharHalliburton.com
Social Media Scheduling	Buffer.com HootSuite.com PostPlanner.com TailwindApp.com
Speaking Assistance	ToastMasters.org
Virtual Meetings & Training	FreeConferenceCall.com Kartra.com Zoom.com
Work for Hire	Fiverr.com TextBroker.com Upwork.com

____

____

____

____

____

____

____

____

Books on Marketing

Title	Author
Entrepreneur Secrets: The New Rules of Wealth Creation	Charlotte Howard
How to Do It Frugally	Carolyn Howard-Johnson
The Christian Writers Market Guide	Steve Laube
The Personal Touch: What You Really Need to Succeed in Today's Fast-Paced Business World	Terrie Williams
Sell Your Book Like Wildfire: The Writer's Guide to Marketing and Publicity	Rob Eager

Tradeshows and Conventions

American Library Association	ALA.org
Book Expo America	BookExpoAmerica.com
Christian Product Expo Show	CPEShow.com
National Religious Broadcasters Conventions	NRB.org
Podfest	PodFestExpo.com

Author Associations

Advanced Writers and Speakers Association	AWSA.com
American Christian Fiction Writers Association	ACFW.com
American Christian Writers	RegAForder.wordpress.com
Christian Authors Network	ChristianAuthorsNetwork.com
Christian Indie Publishing Association	ChristianPublishers.net
Evangelical Christian Publishers Association	ECPA.org
Military Writers Society of America	MWSADispatches.com
National Newspaper Publishers Association	NNPA.org
Nonfiction Authors Association	NonfictionAuthorsAssociation.com
Society of Children's Book Writers and Illustrators	SCBWI.org

Valerie J. Lewis Coleman